Drive and Stroll

Northamptonshire

Barbara Bignell

COUNTRYSIDE BOOKS
NEWBURY BERKSHIRE

To view our complete range of books,
please visit us at
www.countrysidebooks.co.uk

ISBN 1 85306 844 6

For Susan, Steve, Samuel, Julie, Jonathan, Annabel and Oliver

Photographs by the author
Designed by Peter Davies, Nautilus Design

Produced through MRM Associates Ltd., Reading
Typeset by Techniset Typesetters, Newton-le-Willows
Printed by Woolnough Bookbinding Ltd., Irthlingborough

Contents ∂

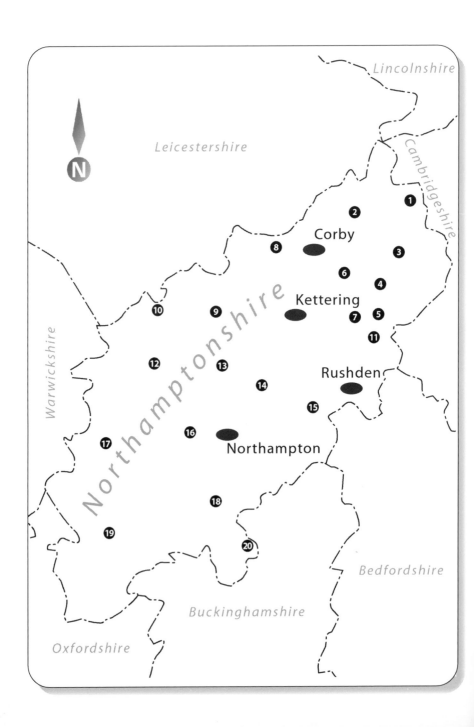

Lincolnshire

Leicestershire

N

Cambridgeshire

❶

❷

Corby

❽   ⬤

❸

❻

❹

Kettering

❼   ⬤   ❺

Warwickshire

❿

❾

Northamptonshire

⓫

⓬

⓭

Rushden

⓮

⬤

⓯

⓰   ⬤

Northampton

⓱

⓲

⓳

⓴

Bedfordshire

Buckinghamshire

Oxfordshire

Contents 𝓮

PUBLISHER'S NOTE

We hope that you obtain considerable enjoyment from this book; great care has been taken in its preparation. Although at the time of publication all routes followed public rights of way or permitted paths, diversion orders can be made and permissions withdrawn.

We cannot, of course, be held responsible for such diversion orders and any inaccuracies in the text which result from these or any other changes to the routes or any damage which might result from walkers trespassing on private property. We are anxious, though, that all details covering the walks are kept up to date and would therefore welcome information from readers that would be relevant to future editions.

The simple sketch maps that accompany the walks in this book are based on notes made by the author whilst checking the routes on the ground. However, for the benefit of a proper map, we do recommend that you purchase the relevant Ordnance Survey sheet covering your walk: the sheet number of the OS Landranger series is given at the beginning of each chapter. Ordnance Survey maps are widely available, especially through booksellers and local newsagents.

Introduction

Northamptonshire is a county of unexpected delights – so much beauty and interest is hidden away behind the trunk roads and motorways. As a resident of just three years and one who had mainly driven through the county in the past, I wondered how I was going to do justice to the project. With so many surprises, both historical and scenic, however, this has been a great learning curve, and one I have thoroughly enjoyed!

The county is rich in history and legends, with many of its grand houses still used as family homes as well as being open to the public. There are antique shops to explore, farmers' markets to visit, and even a Victorian teashop at Thrapston. In addition, the county has over a hundred professional artists, including sculptors, painters, potters, and ceramicists. The Shires Shopping Village alone (north of Weedon) offers a choice of 23 exclusive shops and boutiques. And there are the cosy country pubs with special Sunday roasts, plus the church where water and squash are left out for thirsty visitors. All this, and the peaceful footpaths have not even been mentioned yet.

Annual events in Northamptonshire include scarecrow festivals at Harpole and Aldwincle, the annual World Conker Championships at Ashton, and, for those who like a challenge, there is the International Waendel Weekend near Wellingborough, at which more than 5,000 visitors take part in walking, cycling, and swimming.

I have been reminded of the decisive battle of the civil war at Naseby, of a local association with the gunpowder plot, and the work of the navvies on the railways and canals, not to mention the people who quarried iron ore and manufactured iron and steel. There are those who toiled on the land and especially those who tanned leather and made boots and shoes, for which the county is famous. In recent years, the practice of some of these crafts and occupations has been revived, providing an attraction for tourists and a certain amount of employment for modern Northamptonshire.

It's true there are no mountains to climb here; the highest point in Northamptonshire, Arbury Hill, at 224 metres, is not too far from the Fawsley and Badby walk. With over 80 church spires and 200 medieval churches though, the county is not lacking in attractive heights of a different kind. And going for a stroll rather than striding out does give you a chance to appreciate the countryside in all its aspects.

My problem was selecting just 20 walks from such a variety of locations. In a county with six country parks, more than 80 pocket

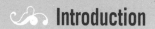

parks, footpaths by the river Nene, quiet towpaths along the Grand Union Canal, and some handsome reservoirs, the opportunities for a stroll are never-ending. Nevertheless, choices were made and the book invites you to walk beside the river Nene, on the way from Wadenhoe to Aldwincle; ramble over parkland landscaped by Capability Brown at Fawsley, with a walk through bluebell woods; stroll across scenic pastureland overlooking the Nene Valley, near Great Doddington; and enjoy the woodland and hedgerows at Fermyn Woods Country Park. Then, for a spot of birdwatching or just a pleasant stroll, you can't beat Summer Leys Nature Reserve – and you will notice that water, always an attraction, is never too far away.

The aim has been to find a stroll with something of special interest, either on the route or nearby. It's even possible to navigate a buggy and young children around parts of Brixworth and Fermyn Woods country parks, following ready-made trails with arrows that youngsters can follow. Whether the playground or ice cream comes before or after the walk could be negotiable!

Mileages given are approximate. Except for the country parks themselves, you need good strong footwear, as some walks can be muddy in wet weather. Needless to say, a waterproof may also be required. A daysack is a good idea for carrying drinks, lunch, snacks, and spare clothing, and, although a sketch map is provided for each walk, an Ordnance Survey map can get you out of trouble if you stray from the track or wish to lengthen the circuit. When compiling these drives and strolls, I have taken into account that many will be walking in a family group. So I have tried to start the routes at places where there is ample parking plus, if possible, the provision of toilets and refreshment kiosks. In some cases, therefore, I have used pay and display car parks, but the charges here are minimal and I'm sure you will feel the amenities they offer will justify the modest expense.

Writing this book has given me great pleasure but it couldn't have happened without the encouragement of my family and friends, as well as the residents of Northamptonshire I've met along the way. Thanks go to all, especially Valerie Back for her support over the years; John Gilpin, Dorothy, Elizabeth Harris, and Pia Bellamy for their company; Hilary Monks and the other Rangers at Fermyn Woods County Park; as well as Ordnance Survey, and Gelert and Coleman for maps and outdoor gear. Safe and happy strolling!

Barbara Bignell

1 Nassington and Yarwell

Yarwell Lock and caravan park

The Walk 3 miles **Terrain** Mainly level, grass footpaths and a byway
Map OS Landranger 142 Peterborough (GR 067962)

How to get there

Nassington is close to the Cambridgeshire border and about 8 miles from Peterborough. Country lanes to the village can be reached from the A43, A47, A605, and A427. **Parking** For patrons, the Black Horse Inn; otherwise, roadside parking is possible.

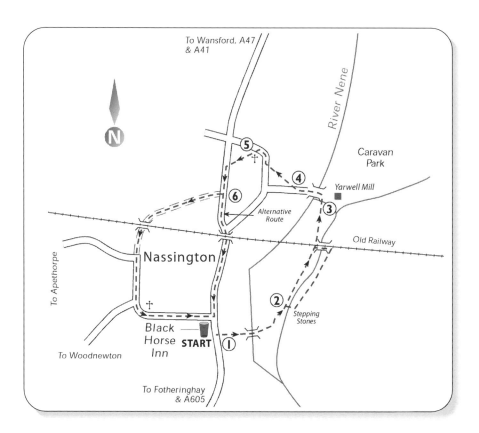

Introduction

Starting off along the Nene Valley Way, the route goes across farmland, beside a stretch of the river, and then over crop fields into Yarwell, which has some lovely limestone cottages, both old and new. The Angel pub in the village looks as though it would fit in your rucksack. An old byway comes next, which can be muddy in wet weather but otherwise makes a pleasant wide stretch between hedgerows. The alternative is to continue on the road back to Nassington and through the main street.

Nassington is close to the county border: a stretch of the river Nene near here is the dividing line between Northamptonshire and Cambridgeshire. The Romans settled in the area, excavating ironstone at Nassington. Clay and limestone for building purposes have come from Yarwell and, in more recent years, gravel has been extracted.

The 13th-century prebendal manor house at Nassington, is the oldest inhabited house in Northamptonshire and stands on an Anglo-Saxon site.

Now part of the Prebendal Manor Medieval Centre, the house and gardens can be viewed, and there are fun activities for children, such as dressing up. (Enquiries: 01780 782575) In 1794, thirteen buildings in Church Street Nassington were destroyed when a fire, started by a boy shooting pigeons, spread from a haystack. Unfortunately, the villagers were away at a feast in nearby Fotheringhay and were unable to stop the devastation. Another feature of the village disappeared in 1981 when the railway bridge was demolished. This was not altogether as a result of the cuts by Dr Beeching in 1966, the station at Nassington having already been closed to passenger traffic in 1957. It should be added, however, that life in the village today is flourishing, with a family butcher's shop, a wine shop, and the well stocked Nassington Stores – a shop, post office and newsagent's in one – in addition to the Black Horse Inn.

With Yarwell mill and lock at about the halfway stage and then the river with cruisers and narrowboats to admire, this is an interesting stroll. The mill dates back to the early 18th-century, though the present three-storey building dates from 1831. (Bank holidays – and weekends in the high season – are very busy times around here.)

For anyone staying at the caravan park at Yarwell, the halfway point could be the Black Horse Inn at Nassington.

The Black Horse Inn

This 17th century listed building in Nassington has a restaurant, garden, and one twin-room B&B. The landlords serve a variety of English and Danish 'fresh own cooked food', including bar snacks, vegetarian, and a children's menu. Opening times: normal pub hours, except between October and March, when it is closed at lunchtime on Wednesday. To order a meal for when you return, ring 01780 782324.

Alternatively, **The Angel at Yarwell** is a small, stone-built pub with low beams and horse brasses; it has served residents of the village for something like 300 years. Telephone: 01780 782582

THE WALK

Just across the road, slightly right from The Black Horse Inn, there's a board with a map of the area. Cross the stile to its right, with signs pointing out the **Nene Valley Way**. The route starts off on a wide grassy track through a field. Bear left, following the Nene Way signs, and then go up the slope, through a gate, and over the bridge across an arm of the Nene. At the other side of the bridge, still showing the Nene Way sign, go over a stile and then ahead along the side of a field to another stile beside a gate. Cross the next field on the clear

The Black Horse Inn at Nassington

way. A gate can be clearly seen at the other side of this field. Cross the stile here, by a post denoting the Nene Way, and shortly after negotiate another gate and stile. Go ahead on the well-defined path.

 ②

There is a choice of routes now. One arrow points forward, keeping the river and hedgerow to the right; the other leads across the river by way of a series of stepping stones (all very exciting if you like a challenge, but my advice is to continue ahead, with the river on the right). The next landmark on the right is an old bridge that once carried a railway line. (Any brave soul taking to the stepping stones should also arrive via the bridge.)

Continue forward along the well-defined path; over to the left cruisers and narrowboats can be seen along the Nene. A thicket, with a kissing gate at each end, brings you to the lock, where caravans come into view.

 ③

Walk over the lock and two more bridges (the Nene Way signs are clear) and then go left past the old mill; keep to the left of the farm buildings, coming out at the drive leading to the reception office of **Yarwell Mill Caravan Park**.

 ④

The footpath is then picked up again at a stile on the right, high on the grassy bank of the drive.

Drive and Stroll

Carry on along the edge of one field and follow the path across the next and over a stile into **Yarwell** village. At the road, turn right and bear left through the village, disregarding the Nene Way to the right, and passing the 13th century church. Almost opposite the church is the **Angel Inn**; continue past, or stop for refreshment.

 ⑤

Just after the church, turn left on a public footpath between two houses and go over a stile. Continue along the edge of a field and over another stile. Then turn right, going alongside a playing field to the road. Turn left along the pavement, keeping a look out for the byway sign on the opposite side of the road and ignoring a farm track. (If you don't fancy the byway, which could be wet and rutted, just carry straight on into Nassington village.)

 ⑥

If using the byway, turn right. At the end, the route goes ahead past houses and **Eastfield Crescent** and at the signpost turns left towards and past the church and more, attractive cottages back to the **Black Horse**.

PLACES OF INTEREST NEARBY

St Mary and All Saints' church, Fotheringhay
This splendid 15th century former collegiate church overlooks the Nene Valley. It has a secret room and some interesting gargoyles.

Nene Valley Railway
Regular services are run throughout the year from Wansford to Peterborough, via Stibbington. Steam trains and diesels trains run, as well as 'Thomas'. Enquiries: 01780 784444 or visit them on line at www.nvr.org.uk, where a full timetable is included.

The Prebendal Manor House at Nassington
The manor is steeped in history: there is a recreated medieval garden to visit; you can learn about the Prebends; and about the archaeological excavations. The manor is open (a charge is made) on Wednesdays, Sundays and bank holiday Monday afternoons from Easter bank holiday until the end of September. There is also a tearoom.

2 Bulwick and Willow Brook

The Queen's Head at Bulwick

The Walk 4 miles **Terrain** Undulating farmland and country lanes, with one marshy spot
Map OS Landranger 141 (GR 965945)

How to get there

From the A43 towards Stamford, turn right for Bulwick 6 miles from Corby. **Parking** The Queen's Head for patrons; there is also roadside parking in this quiet village. The start of the walk is opposite the church on a footpath beside the Queen's Head.

Drive and Stroll

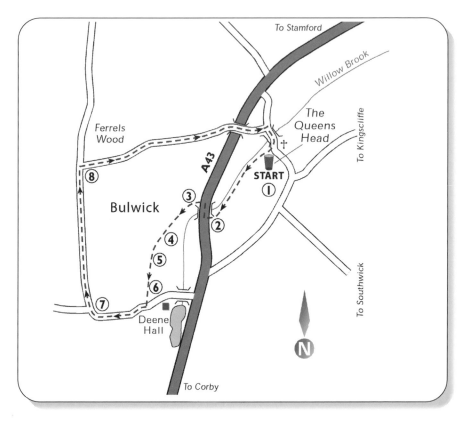

Introduction

Our walk starts off over grassy hills and bumps which are part of a medieval landscape. Then it's alongside fields running parallel with Willow Brook, the second largest tributary of the river Nene, which rises in Corby and joins the Nene at Elton. After crossing the A43, we move down to the other side of the brook and its valley, a delightful area with little bridges and walkways over the marshy parts and only one spot that could call for really tough footwear. Deene village with its thatched cottages comes next, and the rest of the way is along undulating, winding, tarmac lanes with just an occasional vehicle. There is a ford, of the type I remember from years ago, and interesting hedgerows with views across open countryside; if like me you're lucky you may spot deer. Our route then goes over the A43 footbridge and back to Bulwick, past more, attractive cottages.

Pronounced *bullick* (I'm doing my best to learn Northamptonshire pronunciation), the name Bulwick means 'bull farm'. The village has an interesting but somewhat sad history. The intrepid Tryon family lived at Bulwick Hall. Sir George Tryon died in 1893, along with 300 of his men, while he was Commander of the Mediterranean Fleet. During a flawed manoeuvre, his flagship, *Victoria*, was sunk by the battleship *Camperdown* when the two ships collided. The admiral went down with his ship and was reported as saying 'It's entirely my fault', a tragic end to a 45-year naval career. The Tryons also died prematurely on the battlefield. Henry Tryon died aged 25 in command of a night attack at Sebastopol during the Crimean War, and five cousins perished in the Great War; they are commemorated in the medieval church. Another of Bulwick's former residents, Reginald Fitzurse, who had lands in the area during the reign of Henry II, was involved in the murder of Thomas à Becket.

The Queen's Head Inn

This is a comfortable traditional-style country pub in Bulwick, which in the second half of the 17th century was three cottages. It offers a good range of food such as homemade honeyed parsnip soup and Lincolnshire sausage with mustard mash. There are vegetarian choices, sandwiches and a roast on Sunday. Opening hours are Tuesday to Saturday, 12 noon to 2.30 pm and 6 pm to 11 pm and Sunday 12 noon to 3.30 pm. It is closed on Mondays. Telephone: 01780 450272

THE WALK

The route begins over a stile to the side of the **Queen's Head Inn** and goes into parkland with undulations that mark where the village – part of the Bulwick Hall estate – once stood. Walk forward, keeping parallel with **Willow Brook**, which is down to the right. A stile is crossed just to the left of the far corner. Don't go over the bridge on the right, but continue along the edge of a crop field and then bear right.

Don't miss the next stile on the right, just before a copse at the end of a field and down a dip between trees. There are clear footpath signs. Go up the embankment, turn right, and cross the A43 with care. A wooden fingerpost can be seen slightly to the right on the other side of the road.

Cross the stile below the embankment, go over the bridge, and follow the signed and well-defined path. The terrain changes and very pleasantly, winding through the **Willow Brook valley**, with the brook on the left. (Look out for plants that like these damp locations; even in late summer after dry weather, flowers such as comfrey were still blooming.)

 ④

Bear right, away from the brook; the next stile is at a wire fence leading to a large field. This is marshy for a few yards, but you're soon walking forward and slightly upwards away from the damp. Keep going forward across fields and two more stiles, with woodland some way over to the right. (Don't forget to look back at the views as you walk on higher ground.)

 ⑤

An obelisk, the houses of **Deene** village, Deene Hall and Deene church spire come into view, making the way to the village obvious. Head for the rather stylish-looking stone building – the **village hall** – in the corner of the field and over a stile into the village.

 ⑥

Turn right onto the tarmac footpath (or left for the church) and walk through the pleasant village of stone buildings, some of them thatched.

 ⑦

At its end, disregard a footpath sign over on the left and continue round to the right. The terrain changes again, leaving the footpath and taking to the quiet, undulating, winding lanes with firm tarmac. At the signpost, bear right towards **Harringworth** and **Seaton** (Kirby Hall

Bulwick

is to the left). In some place the hedge had been trimmed, giving wide views; at others the blackberries were still tempting.

 ⑧

Turn right by a house at a road junction signed 'Bulwick $1\frac{3}{4}$ miles'. (Alternatively, you could get out the OS map and carry on past **Ferrels Wood** to turn right on a bridleway.) Our route goes along the lane, passing a farm – keep a look out for deer – and then across a footbridge high above the A43. At the T-junction, turn left into **Bulwick**, past thatched cottages; at the next T-junction, turn right onto a tarmac path leading back to the **Queen's Head**.

3 Oundle and Barnwell Country Park

On the way past the marina towards the town

The Walk 3 miles (There are optional waymarked trails around the park of $\frac{1}{3}$ mile, $\frac{2}{3}$ mile, and 1 mile.) **Terrain** All the park walks are level and most, apart from sections of the riverside walk, are hard-surfaced.

Map Landranger 141 Kettering and Corby (GR 035875). A leaflet of the park routes is available from the visitor centre.

How to get there

Follow the brown and white signs from the A605 Oundle bypass. **Parking** At Barnwell Country Park, pay-and-display; entrance to the actual park is free of charge. Free parking for coaches and mini-buses. **By bus** From Oundle town centre, approx. $\frac{1}{4}$ mile from the park entrance. (Enquiries: Travelwise, 01604 236464)

Drive and Stroll

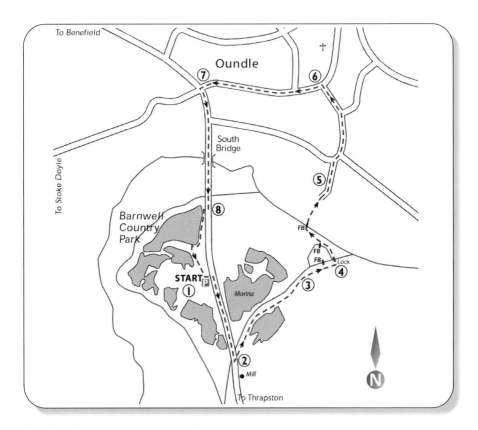

Introduction

Starting in Barnwell Country Park, the first stretch of our route crosses a lock near the marina and then continues over the river Nene and across pastureland, moving into a residential area before reaching the town centre. The return is over a road bridge across the Nene and back into the park. Although the direct route is 3 miles, the possibilites for extra leg-stretching are never-ending, whether around Oundle town, along the river, or by the lakes at Barnwell.

Barnwell Country Park, which arose as result of gravel extraction on the river Nene floodplain, is now an attractive mix of lakes, riverside, meadow, and marshland. The gravel workings were abandoned in the 1960s, which means that Northamptonshire's smallest park has had a chance to mature. You'll find plenty of opportunities for an easy stroll, and possibly spot an otter or a kingfisher, and almost certainly a variety of dragonflies. Wildfowl include coots, moorhens, and swans, as well as winter visitors such as pochard, goosander, and tufted duck. (If you'd like to feed the ducks on Mill Lake, special food – better than bread for both the ducks and the water – is available from the visitor centre.) There's also a children's play area, with equipment for toddlers and older children, and two bird hides with wheelchair access.

The centre of the market town of Oundle has changed little over the last 400 years. A section is now a conservation area, with many impressive town houses. The Talbot Hotel is said to have been built from materials gathered from the destruction of Fotheringhay Castle. The old town hall, originating in 1826, has been restored and now houses the tourist information centre, while the former Congregational church, built in 1864, was opened in 1979 as the Rodolphe Stahl Theatre. Probably the town's most famous asset is its public school, founded in 1556, with its impressive buildings.

It is interesting to note that 200 years ago Oundle had three breweries, and these, plus agriculture, were its main employers. Strolling through the streets on market day (Thursday), I loved the bustling atmosphere and being surrounded by fine buildings and tasteful window displays. A farmers' market is held on the second Saturday of each month, and there are art and antiques shops, as well as 'real' butchers, and bakeries with displays of mouth-watering cakes and savouries – it takes a strong-minded person to walk by and only 'window shop'.

The Mill at Oundle

This pub has a restaurant and bars. It is open seven days a week and offers an extensive and interesting menu, with something to suit every taste. Find out more on www.millatoundle.com. Telephone: 01832 272621.

Alternatively, two other pubs are passed on the route where meals can be taken – **the Angel** and **the Ship**, both in Oundle. The **San Giorgio Ristorante Italiano**, West Street, Oundle, offers a range of Italian food. Telephone: 01832 272720. Light refreshments are also available at the visitor centre in **Barnwell Country Park**. Opening times vary, although the park is open all day every day. Telephone: 01832 273435

THE WALK

①

Leave the car park by the entrance gate and turn right along the tarmac path. Pass the entrance to the Mill at Oundle.

 ②

Opposite **the Mill**, cross the main road with care and locate the clear sign for '**Nene Way** and Footpath **Riverside Walk**'. Bear left on a wide gravel track following the waterside by **Oundle Marina**. With the aid of

Drive and Stroll

Oundle

Nene Way signs and by keeping the river on your left, this is easy to follow. (Keep a look out for herons; we were lucky enough to spot one.)

 ③

Bear left off the main track, still following **Nene Way** signs and the river, but the surface has changed to a wide grass path arriving at a lock. Walk almost to the end.

 ④

Look for a set of steps on the left, just behind the guillotine-type lock, and go over the metal bridge. The footpath is not signed, but the route, slightly to the right, is well marked under foot. Follow this path

to the next bridge over an arm of the Nene. Go over a short stretch of pastureland and across another wider bridge over the river Nene, a lovely spot to pause awhile. A signpost can be seen ahead at the other side of a field with houses to the right. Our walk goes on through the kissing gate towards the town; another sign points right to the Riverside Walk.

 ⑤

Go onwards again, along the pavement, with houses to the right and pastureland to the left. Turn right out of **Bassetford Road**, go over **Herne Road** on the right, and carry on along **St Osyth's Lane**. The spire of the **St Peter's church**

comes into view; and you pass (or enter) a supermarket and **the Angel** public house on your right.

Turn left at the main road, which is **West Street**. (An *Oundle Town Guide* and other information is available from the Tourist Information Centre in West Street.)

Continue through the town and at its end, with a church facing and at a road junction, turn left along the pavement into **Mill Road**, signed 'A605 Kettering and W'Boro'. There is also a sign to

Barnwell Country Park and a garden centre. (The road to the right is marked 'A427 to Corby' – and 'Lyveden New Bield'.)

The route back to **Barnwell Country Park** is straightforward, with a good pathway. Go over the river by the narrow bridge with traffic lights; this is **Barnwell Road**, and it's not long before the sign taking you back into the country park is found on the right.

Enter and turn left along the gravel track for the car park and visitor centre.

PLACES OF INTEREST NEARBY

Lyveden New Bield
Set in glorious open countryside, this lodge or garden house, begun in 1595 by Sir Thomas Tresham, was designed in the shape of a cross. Work on the building stopped in 1605 when Sir Thomas died, and Lyveden, now in the care of the National Trust, has since remained incomplete and virtually unchanged. (Enquiries: 01832 205358)

Ashton
Every year on the second Sunday in October, the green of this picturesque village is the venue for the World Conker Championships, an event attracting competitors from all over the world. Details can be obtained from The Chequered Skipper, telephone: 01832 273494.

Drive and Stroll

4 The Nene Valley at Wadenhoe

Along the River Nene

The Walk $4\frac{1}{2}$ miles **Terrain** A short sharp hill to the church, otherwise gently undulating farmland and meadows
Map OS Landranger 141 Kettering and Corby (GR 015835)

How to get there

Turn off the A605 approximately 4 miles north of Thrapston. **Parking** In the village – next to the recreation hall in Church Street, and at St Michael and All Angels' church, but please consider residents – or at the King's Head (patrons only). **By bus** There are services from Oundle and Thrapston. Saunterbus (a seasonal leisure service) runs on Sundays from April to September. (Enquiries: Traveline, 0870 608 2608)

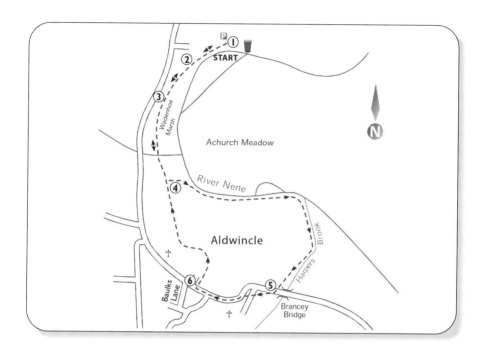

Introduction

From Wadenhoe the walk takes us up the hill past St Michael and All Angels' church, with the river below, along the Nene Way through woodland, beside a meadow, and along the banks of the Nene, passing through Wadenhoe Marsh, a site of special scientific interest. We then go through Aldwincle and follow a field-side path with grand views over the Nene Valley, before retracing our steps to Wadenhoe.

Wadenhoe, with its attractive stone cottages, mill (now a private residence), and a history going back to Saxon times, is surely one of the prettiest and most interesting villages in Northamptonshire. Its name is generally believed to be from the Old English personal name *Wada* and *hoh* 'hill-spur'. On the door of the church, perched on a hill overlooking the river Nene, is information about some of its points of interest. For instance, there is a memorial to the Rt Hon George Ward Hunt, owner of the Wadenhoe estate and Chancellor of the Exchequer in Disraeli's government. He not only brought the first telegraph office to the village to speed his communications with Whitehall, but also built a gasworks in order to light the streets and cottages. As well as admiring the pretty cottages with their thatched, pantiled, or slated roofs, don't forget to visit the dovecote in Pilton Road, where it is

Drive and Stroll

possible to go through the small door to see the interior lined with nesting boxes.

Aldwincle, on a bend of the Nene to the south of Wadenhoe, is recorded in Domesday Book as Eldwincle (from the Old English personal name *Ealda* and *wincel* 'river bend'). Between the two villages, the flood plain of the Nene provides a habitat for all kinds of wildlife. All Saints' church at Aldwincle is a fine-looking building dating back to the 13th century. The carved pinnacled tower, dating to the 15th century, has not been used for a century or more and is now in the care of the Churches Conservation Trust. Inside the church, the furniture has long gone, but the space is used for plays, fund-raising events, and exhibitions; the keyholder lives nearby if you would like to see more. The Old Rectory opposite was the birthplace of John Dryden, Poet Laureate to Charles II.

The King's Head

This 17th century thatched inn at Wadenhoe is located on the banks of the river Nene, near the village hall. It has a reputation for good food and ale in comfortable surroundings. Telephone: 01832 720024

THE WALK

From the **King's Head**, turn left and go through the gate signed '**public footpath and Nene Way**', making for **St Michael and All Angels' church** on the hill. (This is a tarmac path, on a bit of a slope, but as with other inclines on the walk the view of the river and surrounding countryside is well worth the energy expended. Look out for the millennium sundial just before the church.)

From the church, go through the far gate and bear left, following the footpath sign over grass towards woodland. Go down a dip, over a footbridge, and through a kissing gate on the right (**Nene Way**). This takes you through a pleasant wooded area and away from the river.

On reaching the meadow, cross the stile and turn left along a grassy path that is quite well defined. Follow the path round another wooded area, and go over a bridge and squeeze stile on the left. Continue along the edge of a field to a stile and a wide gate.

Turn left at this point, towards the river Nene.

(Wadenhoe Marsh and Achurch Meadow on the opposite bank jointly constitute an SSSI, with waterside meadows and woodland,

24

and marshy grassland providing a habitat for wading birds and many species of flowering plants.)

The church of St Michael and All Angels at Wadenhoe

Next bear right and then left over a stile to the next stretch, which follows the river bank, going over a series of stiles and plank bridges across watercourses of various widths. The river splits in two along the way; our path bends to the right, following **Harper's Brook**, finally alongside a field filled from late spring with a mass of ox-eye daisies, until the roadway is reached, close to **Brancey Bridge**.

 ⑤

Turn right along the **Thorpe Waterville–Aldwincle road** for a short distance. (There is grass verge; and mind the soakaway.) Keep a lookout for a stile on the left; this takes you onto a public footpath across farmland, cutting off the corner of the road, and going over several stiles before emerging just before All Saints' church in Aldwincle.

⑥

Turn left towards the village, going past the church and into **Main Street**. Just after the pocket park (created in 1989 in a former quarry pit and worth visiting for its wealth of wildlife, including red admiral butterflies, green woodpeckers, and rooks), cross the field diagonally and go through a kissing gate and over a footbridge. Two more kissing gates bring you to a well-defined path to the left, which then swings right, along the edge of the field. Continue onwards, enjoying the magnificent view over the river and valley, until the **Nene Way** is reached again. From here, we retrace our route, winding through woodland and bearing right towards the church and car parks.

5 | Historic Thrapston

Thrapston sailing lake

The Walk 4 miles   **Terrain** Easy level walking
Map OS Landranger 141 Kettering and Corby (GR 995785)

How to get there

From A14, take the A6116 to Corby and turn right into Thrapston town centre. Turn down Chancery Lane by Barclays Bank and then left into Meadow Lane. **Parking** Along Meadow Lane. **By bus** There is a bus service from Kettering and a Saunterbus runs at weekends during the summer. (Enquiries: Traveline, 0870 608 2608)

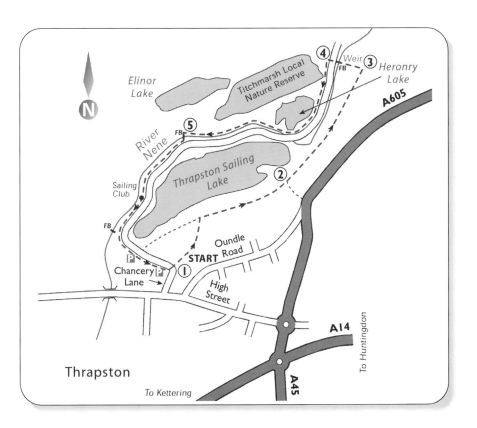

Introduction

Our stroll starts off along the route of the Thrapston Town Walk, going through a woodland arbour, with glimpses of the sailing lake, complete with wild fowl. We then follow part of the old Peterborough to Northampton railway line on our way to the Titchmarsh Local Nature Reserve and a chance to take a look at a tumbling weir. From here our route takes us past Heronry Lake. There follows a stretch beside the river Nene, where the sight of tall teasels and burdock standing up to the breeze and whole swathes of reeds rustling and bending with the wind inspired me to write in my notes 'yet another photograph?' The warm sun and bronze days of autumn with hawthorns bright with berries, many of the leaves carpeting the ground, was quite moving. Spring and early summer must be amazing. The last part of the walk is along a wide gravel track behind the Northampton Sailing Club.

A further stroll around Thrapston is to be recommended. Recorded in *Domesday Book* as Trapestone, this busy market town received its market charter in 1205 from King John. Later, the town was an important stopping point on two 19th century coaching routes. Its role in the transport links of the region continued with the arrival of the Peterborough to Northampton line in 1845, used by passengers until 1964 and for freight until 1972, when the land was purchased by the parish council.

St James' church, dating mainly from the 13th century, is one of the town's oldest buildings. Inside there is a stone tablet bearing the family crest of Sir John Washington, an ancestor of George Washington, the first president of the United States. It is thought that the stars and stripes on this crest provided the inspiration for the American national flag.

The Tasty Bite Victorian Tea Shoppe

Amongst the many attractive shops and cafés in Thrapston is this olde worlde teashop in the High Street, with its ornate cast-iron front. Here the waitresses are clothed in the white cap and black dress of olden days, reminding us of more genteel times. (Next time I'll leave the boots in the vehicle, wash my hands, and comb my hair!) It is open Monday to Friday from 10 am to 5 pm, Saturday 9.30 am to 4.30 pm (closed Sunday). A variety of teas and coffees is offered along with fresh homemade cakes; savouries include pasties, hot sausage rolls and sandwiches.

In addition to the Victorian tea shop, there are several pubs, restaurants, cafés, and shops providing refreshments in Thrapston.

THE WALK

①

Go through the gate marked **Meadow Lane Park** and take the left one of the two wide tracks; a little further on, turn onto the track going right. (The paths on this part of the walk are all well used; it is advisable to stick to the main track through the woodland, keeping the water and wildfowl to the left.)

②

Leave Thrapston Town Walk at the gate and continue ahead and onto the old railway track.

③

At the end, turn left onto another track. Don't panic when you come to a ford with lots of water; there's a footbridge, and the scene is beginning to open up, with a field and sheep to the left. Go over a stile and **Titchmarsh Nature Reserve** is before you. Aldwincle church and village can be seen ahead slightly to the right.

④

At the stile our route goes left. (But, if you appreciate the sight of a rushing weir, turn right for a short way; the white water with its distant village backdrop is well

The Tasty Bite Victorian Tea Shoppe and the Bread Basket at Thrapston

worth a few extra steps.) Having turned left from the stile, it is a matter of continuing ahead, with the river Nene on the left and then the Heronry Lake to the right.

Go through the gate, leaving the Titchmarsh Nature Reserve and turning left over the footbridge. (The Nene Way arrow points forward.) On meeting the tarmac track, turn right, which takes you along the back of the **Northampton Sailing Club**. The Nene is to the right and the spire of Thrapston church appears in the distance. The route is easy to follow, finally bearing left over a bridge with a good view of the sailing boats. Follow the wide track of **Meadow Lane** back to your car, disregarding an entrance to the Thrapston Town Walk.

PLACES OF INTEREST NEARBY

Boughton House, Kettering
Since 1528, Boughton House has been the home of the Dukes of Buccleuch and their Montagu ancestors; it also houses an art collection. The extensive park includes avenues of trees 280 years old, and there are nature trails and places to picnic. The house and park are open during the summer season. Enquiries: 01536 515731.

6 | Fermyn Woods and Rockingham Forest

Fermyn Woods

The Walk 3 miles, with optional detours to viewing points adding a further mile if taken. (There are waymarked alternatives of $\frac{1}{2}$ mile, 1 mile, and $2\frac{1}{4}$ miles.) **Terrain** Undulating with some field walking. The half mile Skylark trail is an easy access route on a hard surface, with seats or resting points at intervals and with gradients of less than 1:20. **Map** OS Landranger 141 Kettering and Corby (however, this doesn't show the many footpaths criss-crossing the park) (GR 955845)

How to get there

From the Brigstock bypass on the A6116 between Corby and Thrapston, follow the brown and white country park signs. **Parking** At Fermyn Woods Country Park, pay and display. Free parking available for mini-buses and coaches. **By bus** There is a regular bus service from Brigstock village. (Enquiries: Travelwise, 01604 236464)

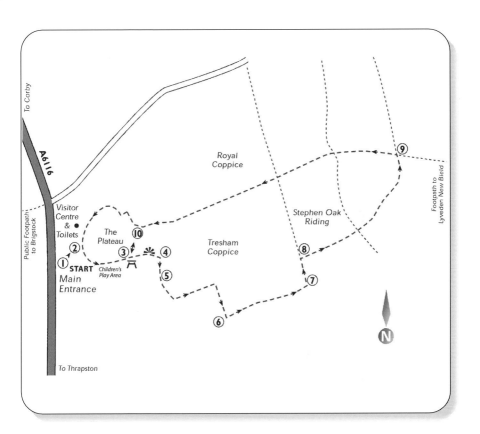

Introduction

This walk of 3 or 4 miles using some of the orange band markers is a little more challenging than the waymarked circular routes, moving out of the park and forest to some field walking with panoramic views. It's as well to wear walking boots or shoes with a thickish sole as some of the forest paths have a covering of quite chunky gravel – which of course can be an advantage in less than perfect conditions.

In 2002 Northamptonshire County Council and the Forestry Commission decided to unite Brigstock Country Park and Fermyn Woods to create Northamptonshire's largest country park: Fermyn Woods Country Park. This a marvellous place for strolls and walks of all types and lengths, with opportunities for spotting a variety of wild flowers, birds, and butterflies. The visitor centre offers hands-on displays, information, souvenirs, park and countryside books, orienteering and discovery packs (telephone: 01536 373625).

Drive and Stroll

The park is located in the heart of the medieval Rockingham Forest, near the village of Brigstock, and is a mixture of scrub, grass meadows, ponds, and woodland. The ancient forest was created by Norman kings to indulge their love of hunting. Now a mixture of broad-leaved and conifer plantations, the woodlands were disafforested in 1650. The plan is to convert the conifer plantations back to semi-natural broad-leaved woodlands. Between 1920 and the 1960s, part of the park was quarried for sand and gravel, used in the building of Corby New Town. The undulating landscape we see in today's park, which opened in 1985 as Brigstock Country Park, was developed from the sandpits.

Although the Brigstock area was settled as far back as the Iron Age, the present village developed from a Saxon settlement in a clearing in Rockingham Forest. The centre of the village is Hall Hill with its circle of stone houses around an ancient market cross, where, since 1466, when Edward IV granted a charter for a weekly market, the village women have sold their produce. The men it seems had other ideas, and at one time or another twelve buildings have been used as public houses. During the reign of Elizabeth I, the village acquired some notoriety as the haunt of deer-stealers, but to its credit Brigstock entered early into education, a school having been endowed there in 1620 by the Rev. Nicholas Latham, the parson of Barnwell, near Oundle. More of the history of Brigstock can be found in the WI publication *Northamptonshire Villages*.

Fermyn Woods Country Park

The visitor centre has vending machines for hot and cold drinks; and sweets, snacks, and ice cream can be purchased. Opening times are 11 am to 5 pm at weekends and during school holidays but otherwise variable.

Refreshments are also available in Brigstock, for instance at **The Green Dragon** public house. Opposite, there is a village shop for picnic supplies.

THE WALK

From the car park, take the path to the visitor centre and information board, where there are details of the optional shorter walks. The ranger also has on display a list itemizing the types of birds, butterflies, etc. to be seen.

Facing away from the information board, disregard the first path on the left, with a red arrow, and take the second, which is a wide gravel track, gently winding upwards, with a children's playground on the right and picnic tables on both sides, and later coming to a small car park for disabled people. Ignore the orange and mauve marker

The children's playground at Fermyn Woods Country Park

posts as you move along. (Note: the red arrow points to the start of a nature trail which goes past Reedy Pond and Long Pond, both of which are seen on the way back.)

Take a bit of a detour if possible: a path on the left gives lovely views of the surrounding countryside, with two churches in the distance. Walk up one of the paths on the mounds to even higher viewpoints. Returning to the main track,

continue forward and very soon you will come to the **Woodland car park** for disabled visitors.

Ahead and soon after the car park, there's a wooden bench on the right, followed by a gate and small bridge, which is crossed to reach one of the field sections of the walk.

Turn left, still going slightly uphill on a wide grassy footpath – but on the outside of the country park and the forest now – with a field in front and to the right, and a panoramic view over Northamptonshire's glorious countryside. At the footpath sign, continue ahead, following the contour of the forest and stopping periodically to look around as the views get even wider. Follow the next footpath arrow, staying on the outside of the forest and bearing right on a well defined path.

Turn left at the next footpath sign and walk down the dip between the hedges and onto another field. Turn left again, with the field on the right, a tall hedge to the left, and woodland in the distance. Continue ahead along this grassy path.

At the next sign, indicating a public bridleway, turn left and go over a wooden sleeper bridge.

Then at an orange band marker post, turn right along a wide grassy bridleway with a plantation of young oaks on the right. At the next orange marker, keep right along the wide track, passing a wooden bridge. This straight stretch is just inside the forest.

Coming almost to the forest road, turn left and keep following the orange bands, which take in some of the most pleasant woodland. At the grassy T-junction, turn right and bear left, ignoring the orienteering sign ahead. Walk some distance through light woodland; eventually you will come to a fence on the left, which separates a brook from the path and a bluebell wood. Continue straight ahead.

As mentioned, the last stretch after leaving the wood is part of the nature trail, with much natural history to enjoy. Pass one pond now. (On my spring visit this was full of water and was thriving but by September it had dried up; a notice mentioned that the area had been fenced off as part of a great crested newt project. Let's hope nature put things back on track when the rains arrived. Along the next stretch the bushes were heavy with plump sloes, hawthorn berries – or what we used to call bread and cheese – and rosehips.) The path then bears right, passing the next little pond, with a picnic table. (This did have some water at the time of my autumn visit, and lots of those tall, rich brown, furry-looking 'bullrushes', which I believe are really called reed mace.)

At the wooden bridge with a concrete pathway, ignore the orange marker to the left and continue down the slope, past the notice board, and back to the visitor centre and car park.

7 Twywell Hills and Dales Nature Reserve

The Old Friar, Twywell

The Walk 3 miles   **Terrain** Gently undulating
Map OS Landranger 141 Kettering and Corby (GR 935775)

How to get there

From the A14 roundabout at the junction with the A510, go towards Cranford St John, and make for the entrance to Twywell Hills and Dales Nature Reserve on the right. **Parking** In the car park just inside the entrance.

Drive and Stroll

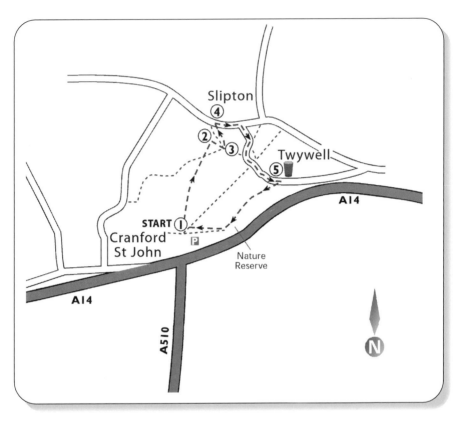

Introduction

The 135-acre Twywell Hills and Dales Nature Reserve has been created from two disused ironstone quarries. After years of iron ore extraction, when the iron was transported by trucks and rail to furnaces at Islip, the site was abandoned during the 1940s and 50s. The area is now an extremely pleasant location for numerous strolls on winding footpaths over undulating terrain. An expanse of woodland adds further variety, and this walk also takes in meadow and farmland. If you are interested in wild flowers and their habitats, this could be the place to explore, especially in springtime. On my autumn ramble, I came across giant thistle heads and rosehips as well as a whole hedgerow of sloes with the brightest blue bloom I've ever seen. The birdsong in the woodland was uplifting, to say the least.

The village of Twywell is fairly long and winding, with attractive stone cottages and houses. We stroll past Macqueen House, headquarters of the Northamptonshire Girl Guide Association, and further along, set back on the right, is a wholesome looking family butcher's and delicatessen. At the church, to be found in Church Lane, of course, there is a piece of bark wrapping reputedly associated with Dr David Livingstone. It is said that when the explorer died his heart was buried in Africa and his embalmed body was wrapped in bark for transportation to England, where it was finally laid to rest in Westminster Abbey. Horace Waller, rector of Twywell at the time, published in 1874 an account of Livingstone's last moments as related to him by Livingstone's faithful servants Susi and Chuma. These two men visited Twywell in that year. (A note on the door of the church gives names of key holders.) The Old Friar public house as well as the signpost back to the Hills and Dales Nature Reserve is at the far end of the village.

The Old Friar

At the far end of Twywell village is the Old Friar. The building is of mellowed stone with low ceilings, open fires, and a welcoming glow on entry. It has a reputation for good food, including grills, bar snacks, interesting vegetarian dishes, and a Sunday roast. There are also special children's menus. Food is available at lunchtime, except on Mondays, and in the evening, during usual opening hours. There is a play area and a small garden. Telephone: 01832 732625.

THE WALK

From the car park, looking across the meadow, go through the kissing gate to the left of the map board and bear left onto the bridleway. Shortly, take the left fork (public bridleway). At a wooden signpost (Cranford to the left), go ahead and at a disc arrrow take the bridleway bearing left. (It is now just possible to hear the buzz of the A14, but it can't be seen.) At the finger post, take the left fork, signed 'public bridleway, Twywell and Slipton'. Then go through a gate into a meadow and cross diagonally – the grassy path is well-defined. The next gate can be seen at the other side. Keep going forward, with the hedge on your right and the field on left. Continue ahead for a short distance, disregarding both a track on the right going into a field and then a plank bridge.

At the last oak tree on this stretch take the right fork – a footpath through a wide gap in the hedge, with a disc sign. (The farm track goes to the left.) Walk ahead along the field edge, with a hedgerow on the left.

At the next oak tree, turn left and go through a metal gate. The

Twywell Hills and Dales Nature Reserve

footpath goes along the left edge of the field.

 ④

At the road, turn right towards **Twywell**. At the bend, ignore the footpath to the left and enter **High Street**, with **Macqueen House** on the right. The sign for the Twywell nature reserve footpath is at the far end of the village, almost opposite the **Old Friar** pub.

 ⑤

A large sign points to a gravel track between houses, leading to allotments. Just before these, take the arrowed footpath on the right at the end of several garages. Then go through a kissing gate and follow the public footpath arrow pointing left. Now go through another gate and down a few steps. Turn right and bear left across a meadow with a well-defined grassy path, making for a gate into woodland, where there is a footpath sign and a map. Go up a flight of about 17 steps now and forward onto a wide track bearing left through woodland. Go over the crossroads on this undulating track between the trees and continue to a T-junction; turn right here and very soon turn left up onto a ridge. Keep ahead now, with views on both sides, coming then to another wooded area. Go down steps on the left and turn right at the bottom. Carry on ahead, and after following a fence round the pond to a gravel path go up the first set of steps. Ignore a second flight on the left, continuing ahead to a gate and an immediate left turn back to the car park.

8 East Carlton Countryside Park

The entrance to Dale Pocket Park from the Jurassic Way

The Walk 3 miles   **Terrain** Undulating, over pasture and through quiet villages
Map OS Landranger 141 Kettering and Corby (GR 835895)

How to get there

Leave the A427, Corby–Market Harborough road, 3 miles west of Corby, following the signs to the country park. **Parking** At East Carlton Countryside Park (free parking).

Drive and Stroll

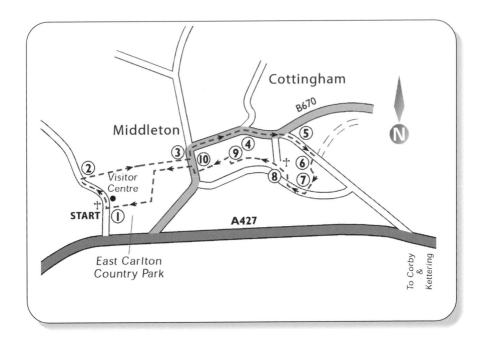

Introduction

There is plenty of variety on this walk taking in a couple of stretches of the Jurassic Way, with wide views over the river Welland into Leicestershire. From East Carlton Country Park, it goes through the quiet villages of Middleton and Cottingham (on pavements) and then, still climbing upwards, across pastureland, with more views, and down through the Dale Pocket Park. The last stretch, back to the countryside park, is easy walking on lanes. Like all circular walks, it could be taken the opposite way round but we prefer this, as the Dale Pocket Park makes for perfect strolling in this direction.

East Carlton Countryside Park lies on the edge of the Welland Valley, just inside the Northamptonshire boundary, and is managed by Corby Borough Council. It offers numerous strolls through mature woodland and grassland. Part of the Jurassic ironstone rock seam which extends from Dorset to Yorkshire runs through the parkland, and an outcrop can be seen on the trails. The presence of this seam accounts for the establishment and development of the Corby iron and steel industry, which is portrayed in the Steel Heritage Centre housed in the old coach house of rather grand-looking East Carlton Hall. As well as the steel display, the showcase with minerals, fossils, and archaeological remains is very instructive. Also not to be missed are the upstairs workshops where individual craftsmen demonstrate their skills. The hall itself, built in 1863, is unfortunately not open to the public, but it is worth taking a walk around the perimeter.

Dotted around the park are large pieces of machinery reminding us of the steel industry, and on my last visit blacksmith Alan Cairney was busy demonstrating his craft in the New Forge. The countryside park is open all year round; in winter the gates close at 4 pm and in summer at 8 pm. (Telephone 01536 770977)

The Spread Eagle

This family orientated pub in Cottingham offers good pub food such as steaks, pies, fish dishes, and vegetarian options. They are open Monday to Thursday from 11.30 am to 3 pm and 6 pm to 11 pm. On Friday, Saturday, and Sunday they are open all day. Food is served every day from 12 noon to 2 pm and 6 pm to 9 pm, except Sunday when food is served from 12.30 pm to 8 pm. Telephone: 01536 772038. There is also a village shop in Cottingham.

Alternatively, **the cafeteria at East Carlton Countryside Park** is warm and friendly, and is open all year round, offering a wide range of light meals, hot and cold drinks, cakes, and ice cream, which can be enjoyed inside or outside in the sheltered courtyard. Opening times vary. Telephone: 01536 770977

THE WALK

Leave the car park by the main gate and turn right along the pavement, with the church across the road. Ignore a drive on the right (house only) and follow the lovely old stone wall, not forgetting to look over the wall to the rolling hills.

Soon after the speed limit sign, turn right over a stile and onto the **Jurassic Way**. This takes you along a signed, well-defined path through a series of stiles and kissing gates for about a mile, following the outside edge of the park, with wide views to the left and woodland with birdsong to the right. After the last kissing gate, as houses on the edge of **Middleton** come into sight, continue ahead and cross a wooden sleeper bridge, which keeps your feet out of a patch of marshy ground.

On reaching the road, **The Red Lion** public house will be seen on the opposite side. Turn left along the pavement, leaving the Jurassic Way, and at the road junction bear right into **Main Street** and walk through the attractive village of **Middleton**.

At the junction signed 'B670

Drive and Stroll

Rockingham', turn right up a hill and go past **Hunting Lodge Hotel** on your right. Further along you'll come to the inviting **Spread Eagle** family pub, offering, among other facilities, freshly cut sandwiches and a variety of hot meals.

At the **Cottingham village sign**, with the village shop and post office on your right, turn right along the old Roman road, signed 'Corby and Kettering'.

Walk along the pavement and cross where necessary for safety, ignoring a footpath near a metal gate over to the right. At the top of the hill, just before the end of the built-up area sign, turn right at the footpath pointer, over a stile into a field. Cross diagonally, negotiating a few undulations which are the result of ancient ridge and furrow ploughing. Cross another two fields now, moving uphill slightly all the time; the route is obvious. Don't forget to look back from time to time; the view is worth every puff and gasp. Keeping the hedge to your right, turn right just past a stile made from a railway sleeper

This pump is to be found at Middleton

and walk over a fourth field, which brings you out to the road.

Turn right along the road, go past a farm gate, followed by a stile, and turn right through a kissing gate into the **Dale Pocket Park**. Bearing left, stroll along the path that can be clearly seen at the centre of the dip, with grassy areas on each side, and enjoy this fine example of a pocket park, away from the cares of the world.

Go straight ahead and through the gate at the end of the park. Turn left here to rejoin the **Jurassic Way**. The footpath runs behind several gardens, with hillside views between the houses. (For a closer look at the lovely church of **St Mary the Virgin**, walk ahead, following the public footpath sign.)

After the first upward slope, the footpath levels out, with great views to the right. Soon, as another reward, our route goes downhill and then along a gravel lane. (At the T-junction, notice the old water pump ahead.) Turn right down **School Hill**, which is quite exciting in a way because it is so steep.

At the end, turn right (the **Red Lion** is to the right) and look for the footpath to **Wilbarston** on the left, opposite the Red Lion sign. We now retrace our steps into East Carlton Countryside Park, turning left off the Jurassic Way at any of several points (the choice is yours). Carry on down towards the cafeteria, craft workshops, forge, the heritage centre, and car park.

PLACES OF INTEREST NEARBY

Rockingham Castle
Lying 2 miles north of Corby on the A6003, Rockingham Castle was built by William the Conqueror; it was a royal fortress for 450 years and has been a family home since 1544. The beautifully furnished rooms and 12 acres of gardens are open to the public at various times; there is also a gift shop. Enquiries: 01536 770240

9 Kelmarsh, Brampton Valley Way and the Oxenden Tunnel

One of the detours from the route at B V Way

The Walk $4\frac{1}{2}$ miles **Terrain** Easy walking along wide, well-defined tracks, with an undulating path through woodland
Map OS Landranger 141 Kettering and Corby (GR 745805)

How to get there

From A14, take the A508 towards Market Harborough; slightly north of Kelmarsh, turn right at a sign for Arthingworth. **Parking** Kelmarsh Tunnel car park, which is on the left, just past the railway bridge.

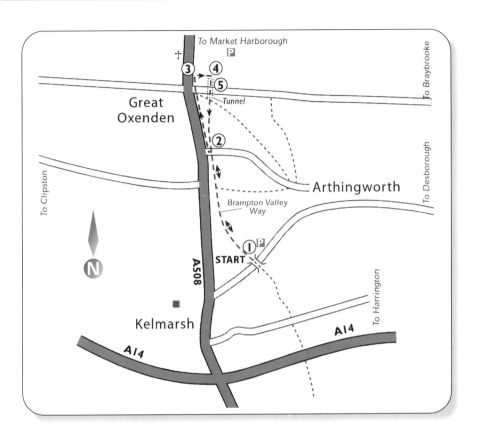

Introduction

This stroll along a section of the Brampton Valley Way must be one of the easiest in the book, though not the shortest. The track along the old railway line between Northampton and Market Harborough is wide and level, curving its way between lines of hedges and trees, which in autumn are a riot of colour, and there are several seats along the way. Through the many gaps in the hedgerows, there are views of open countryside with cornfields and grazing sheep, and along one stretch the route winds its way up and down through woodland, complete with a trickling stream.

For some, the highlight of the stroll will be the walk through Oxendon Tunnel, though for anyone not keen on around 400 metres of darkness, the pavement on the edge of the village of Great Oxendon can be used in both directions. Daylight can be seen at the end of the tunnel, and there are reflectors on the walls, but it's best to take a good torch. After the tunnel, the

Drive and Stroll

last section is a matter of retracing one's boot prints back to the car park or possibly lengthening the walk to the Bull's Head in Arthingworth.

The Brampton Valley Way is a 14 mile linear walk. (It is also a cycleway; so be prepared.) A stretch of the line is still being used by the Northampton and Lamport Railway, and Pitsford and Brampton station at Chapel Brampton is open on selected days in the main season.

The Bull's Head

Situated in the hilltop village of Arthingworth, the Bull's Head provides food at lunchtime and in the evening, and at lunchtime on Sunday. Coffee and tea are also available. Telephone: 01858 525637

Alternatively, there is **the George, Great Oxendon**, which was awarded four crowns by the English Tourism Council. There is a restaurant, bar, conservatory and gardens.

THE WALK

①

From the car park, take the steps up to the **Brampton Valley Way** and turn right along the main track. If you would rather not use steps, there is a gradual slope (a bridleway) to the right. (One of the first 'official' resting points is at the entrance to **Triangular Meadow**, with a seat facing the sun, if we're lucky.)

After about a mile a signpost tells us that Clipstone is $1\frac{1}{4}$ miles to the left, Northampton 13 miles in the direction we have come from, and, if we keep on past Oxendon Tunnel, Market Harborough is $3\frac{1}{4}$ miles. The next signpost tells us we've walked $1\frac{1}{2}$ miles. If you would like lunch and a detour, Arthingworth and the Bull's Head is $1\frac{1}{4}$ miles to the right.

②

At the signpost here turn left onto a pavement beside the road, where we turn right towards **Great Oxendon**.

For much of the time the tarmac path at the edge of the village is set a little way back from the A508. On the opposite side of the road, the scene is one of open countryside with grazing livestock. Roughly level with the 40 mph road sign, over to the right on a hill, the ventilation shaft of Oxendon Tunnel can be seen.

Going into the village, continue ahead over **Braybrooke Road** and past or into the **George Inn**, stopping perhaps to look at the large plaque to commemorate the millennium. (Those not wishing to go through Oxendon Tunnel may want to retrace their steps from this point.)

 ③

Turn right down a drive just before

46

Oxenden Tunnel from the Kelmarsh end

a row of houses. On the right of the drive, there is a stile and a wooden fingerpost pointing to Braybrook. Walk a short way forward and turn left over a stile marked '**Jurassic Way**', crossing a field to the next stile, which is easily located. (The stables can be seen in a dip to the right.) The next stile can be spotted in a tree-dark corner at the far left of the field.

 ④

Turn left (ignoring the Jurassic Way, which bears right) onto a narrow path winding its way down through woodland. Before long a bridge on the Brampton Way comes into view but don't get too carried away looking at the bridge. At the bottom is a small shallow stream, barely 18 inches wide, which you cross by way of some wooden poles. Then turn right to go through **Oxendon Tunnel**. If you don't wish to go through the tunnel, retrace your steps from point 2.

 ⑤

On leaving the tunnel, retrace your steps along the **Brampton Valley Way** to the car park.

10 The Grand Union at Welford

Welford Wharf

The Walk 5 miles   **Terrain** Level walking on towpath; then undulating farmland
Map OS Landranger 140 Leicester (GR 645805)

How to get there

On the north side of Welford, turn off the A5199 at a sign for British Waterways Welford Wharf. **Parking** At Welford Wharf, in the free parking area beyond Wharf Inn car park. **By bus** There are services from Northampton, Leicester, and Market Harborough. (Enquiries: Traveline, 0870 608 2608)

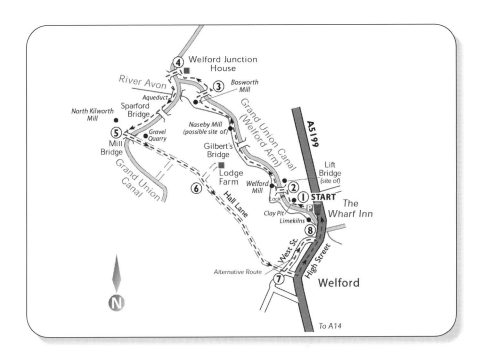

Introduction

The walk starts off along the towpath of the Welford arm of the Grand Union Canal, turning onto the main waterway, and then through farmland. After a longish farm-drive midway, there's a choice of routes on the way back to the starting point. On display panels near the limekilns, alternative routes are described for shorter walks of 2 and 3 miles or, for the energetic, longer ones of 6 and 8 miles. Our 5-mile route is no boring straight canal stroll, however: around nearly every bend there is something that shouts 'Photograph!', whether a stretch of unspoilt countryside, a barn across the way, or the seasonal changes in foliage and flora.

Located halfway between Leicester and Northampton, Welford was an important stopping place in coaching days, with seven coaching houses or inns along the high street. The most famous in its time was The Talbot Inn, immortalized by Charles Dickens in *Bleak House*.

The Grand Union Canal brought business to the village when, in 1814, the Welford arm was added to the main waterway. The George Inn (renamed The Wharf Inn around 1947) was a well-known trading centre for coal, coke, granite, and salt; at one time up to 1,000 tons of coal was stored in the yard. It was run by the Gilbert family, and in 1904 when her husband, William, died

Drive and Stroll

Mary Gilbert, mother of two daughters, not only ran the inn but also ferried the goods on her narrowboat, *Gwen Mary*.

Brickmaking also took place in the village; the site of the clay pit is now a marina, and the area where the bricks were made is its car park. Lime in various forms was another local product, and the limekilns at Welford Wharf have been partly restored. The story of lime and its uses is displayed on information boards near the kilns, which can be visited free of charge.

The 13th century church of St Mary was originally a chapel of ease for nearby Sulby Abbey. The abbey was a casualty of Henry VIII's dissolution, but it is said that a secret tunnel linked the church and the abbey and that ghostly echoes from the passage can be heard in the fields close by.

Welford Wharf is in Northamptonshire, but if you walk a few steps in certain directions you are in Leicestershire. A bridge over the river Avon, close to the wharf, marks the boundary. It should be noted that the route goes through a species-rich wildlife habitat which is being encouraged to flourish and is protected under the Countryside Stewardship Scheme. Access to the Avon floodplain is provided until 2008. For more information, read the signboards at Welford Lock and bridge 41.

The Wharf Inn

This is a traditional local in Welford offering good English home-cooked food, such as local ham and chips, and fillet steak. Opening times are Tuesday to Friday from 12 noon to 2.30 pm and 6 pm to 9 pm, and all day Saturday. There is a Sunday carvery from 12 noon to 3.30 pm, but the inn is closed on Sunday evening and all day Monday. Children are welcome and there is a children's menu. Dogs, on a lead and under control, are allowed in the bar only, and there is a garden. Telephone: 01858 575075

Alternatively, the Elizabethan Inn and Restaurant in the High Street, Welford, is open from 12 noon to 2.30 pm and from 5.30 pm to 11 pm on weekdays, and all day on Saturday and Sunday. Telephone: 01858 575311

THE WALK

From the lime kilns, turn left along the gravel towpath, going past the toilets (which may be locked). Very soon you will see lots of narrowboats lining the bank and in the marina. Walk around the marina and pick up the canal path at the other side. (On the opposite side of the canal there are fields.) Very soon **Welford Lock** is reached.

Turn left over the lock bridge and immediately right along the grass path by the canal. Continue ahead, past the wooden bridge.

50

On the route

 ③

At the **brick bridge** with a farm to the left, cross over and go through a gate to the path along the opposite side of the canal.

(Further along, a signpost, obviously meant for canal traffic, tells us we have come $1^3/_4$ miles from Welford; Norton Junction is $15^1/_4$ miles to the left; and Foxton is $7^3/_4$ miles ahead.)

 ④

Turn left over **bridge no. 42**, which is at the junction with the main Grand Union Canal, and turn left again, over a stile, and then walk along the other bank, bearing right on the towpath of the Grand Union.

(There are attractive undulating country views with a patchwork of fields along this stretch. A row of tying-up points probably indicates that this is a busy spot in the holiday season. The towpath is quite wide, though.)

After passing under **bridge 41**, continue ahead along the reed-lined path to **bridge 40**, which is about the halfway mark of this walk.

 ⑤

Turn left over the bridge (there is no sign). You are now on a grass bridleway going along the side of a field and climbing uphill with views all round, of reservoirs in one direction and of several church spires. Continue ahead, bearing right on the same track, which changes to a gravel surface, and passing a public bridleway disc. At the point where the bridleway goes

Drive and Stroll

to the left, we walk forward onto a grass track signed **Mary Gilbert Walk**.

At the concrete roadway, carry on ahead and downhill, ignoring the left turn to the farmhouse. This stretch passes several thickets before houses start to come into sight. Ignore the footpath over a footbridge to the left (Welford Walk) and carry on forward, passing some smart cottages on the left.

At the T-junction, turn left towards the church. Now comes the choice: either turn right, coming shortly to **High Street**, along which you pass (or enter) the Elizabethan Inn, before turning left, back to the Wharf; or continue along **West Street**, which runs parallel.

(The latter is probably the easier of the two, but I found the houses and cottages in High Street interesting and so different in style; also there is a licensed shop selling chocolate bars, crisps, ice cream, and other snack foods. The pavement is not very wide, though, and the traffic can be intimidating.)

At the end of **High Street**, just past the end of West Street, turn left into the **Wharf and Canal Pocket Park**, which is a conservation area. This is taken good care of by local volunteers, and a noticeboard gives a list of wild flowers to be found there. The pocket park cuts off a busy corner of the road and leads through a garden with ponds and benches where you can sit and enjoy the scene. Cross two footbridges then to get back to the wharf.

PLACES OF INTEREST NEARBY

Welford and Sulby reservoirs
Reached from the Naseby road, these were built to supply water to the main canal via the Welford arm.

Naseby
The battlefield, 3 miles south-east of Welford, was the scene in 1645 of a decisive encounter in the first phase of the Civil War, in which the royalist army under Prince Rupert was routed by Cromwell's forces. Two monuments are claimed to mark the battle site: the Naseby monument, erected in 1936 on the west side of Sibertoft Road outside Naseby village, and the Naseby obelisk, erected in 1823 on the east side of Clipston Road, also outside village. There is a lay-by at the latter.

Ringstead and Kinewell Lake

Spring is on the way at Brightwells Lake

The Walk 3 miles, or 4 miles with village. Circuit of Kinewell Lake, about $1\frac{1}{2}$ miles. **Terrain** Some road-walking, but mainly over grassy, level paths
Map OS Landranger 141 Kettering and Corby (GR 985755)

How to get there

At Raunds roundabout, leave the A45 Thrapston–Northampton road on a minor road, signed Ringstead. On reaching the village, turn left and drive on past the church. The entrance to Kinewell Lake car park is at the far end of the village. **Parking** At Kinewell Lake Nature Reserve.

Drive and Stroll

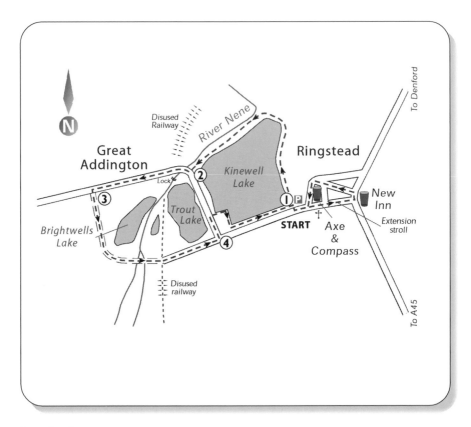

Introduction

Leaving the car park, we follow a grassy path round Kinewell Lake. Soon we are joined on the right by the river Nene and narrowboats with romantic names like *African Queen* or more puzzling names such as *Oodunit*. We then arrive at a lock on the river for a spot of gongoozling (or, more prosaically, watching boats pass through the lock), before leaving the river and continuing across farmland to Brightwell Lake, alive with the sounds of coots and gulls, and a lily pond beyond. More wildlife-rich lakeside scenes follow as we make our way to Ringstead for refreshments before returning to the starting point. There are some stretches of road on this walk, but few vehicles on my visits, and the views over the lakes and the valley certainly compensate.

It is 30 years since gravel was extracted from the Kinewell Lake area, which means that it has had time to mature into an interesting and relaxing place to stroll. We have the local parish council – and, I'm sure, many others – to thank for the planting of more than 1,500 trees and shrubs on the 50 acres of flooded pits and 80 acres of adjacent meadows. Unlike many gravel pits along the valley, Kinewell is connected to the Nene, thus allowing fish to migrate between the two.

Many of the buildings in Ringstead were constructed from the local ironstone. Most were built in the 17th and 18th centuries, but you can't miss the oldest building, the church of the Nativity of the Blessed Virgin Mary, which dates back to the 13th century. The village bears the distinction of having been the birthplace of Alf Roberts, the father of Margaret Thatcher. It seems that some of her forebears, like many villagers in Northamptonshire, were shoemakers, working in their homes or village halls.

The Axe and Compass

As a notice board proclaims, this country pub at Ringstead offers 'quick and easy meals at affordable prices'. There is a varied menu, including vegetarian, and food can be eaten in the restaurant as well as the bar (which also offers skittles and darts). There is a garden with children's swings. It is advisable to book. Telephone: 01933 622227

THE WALK

From Kinewell Nature Reserve car park, take the right-hand grassy path going round the lake. (There is a noticeboard to the right giving the lake's history.) The water soon comes into view, and reappears at intervals. The path becomes narrower, and, continuing round the lake, you come to a seat and then a little detour to a raised grassy patch by the lakeside.

(Stop awhile at this 'oh so quiet and soothing' place to absorb the atmosphere. I wandered around taking photographs of the light on the water, trying to include a bird as it swooped over the water.)

Continue on the circuit path into a wooded area and over a short wooden walkway. The river now appears on the right, and the route continues parallel with the river along a wide grassy stretch between the lake and the river. As **Ringstead Lock** and a bridge appear, go over a wooden stile to the road. (Although this walk doesn't include the lock, who can resist watching as a boat negotiates a lock, or, as canal users would say, being a 'gongoozler'.)

Turn right across a stone bridge over the river Nene and pass **Willy Watt Mill**, once a working watermill. The next stretch is beside the Great Addington road. The path peters out, but it is possible to

Drive and Stroll

Brightwells Lake from the Great Addington road

walk along a grass verge in places. (Over to the left a view of the Nene, Brightwells Lake, and several church spires soon appears; there is a passing place where you can stand to admire it.) Disregarding any gaps in the hedge that look as though they could be the start of a footpath, continue round several bends in the road until you come to a wide green gate on the left.

 ③

Cross the road and go towards **Brightwells Lake** down the wide track between farmland. At the bottom of the hill, bear right, keeping the lake on your left (though you may decide to take a closer look). Leaving the lake, you'll come to a wooden bridge, which

you cross; keep walking onwards over several bridges and through car parks used by anglers, with **Upper Ringstead Lock** to the right. Still walking ahead, look out for a swan's nest on the right and a pond with waterlilies on the left. Continue on the gravel track and tarmac lane past the trout and salmon fishery on the left.

 ④

You'll arrive at a T-junction (more like a Y-junction, really) at a bend in the main road; turn left and cross over to a squeeze stile leading back to Kinewell Lake. Take the track bearing right, which goes along the side of the lake, with more vantage points. The church spire then comes into view.

If this encourages you to lengthen the walk, turn left out of the car park and continue towards the church. (Take the second left turn for the Axe and Compass.) Go across **Chapel Street**, and at the junction by the New Inn turn left into **High Street**, where you will find an interesting mix of architectural styles. Pass the village hall on the left, a playground and then a supermarket and the post office.

Keep straight ahead, crossing the other end of **Chapel Street**, and then turn left into **Carlow Road**, passing a farm on the right before going past or into the **Axe and Compass**. To return to the car park, either walk to the end of the road and turn right, or (to avoid pavements) cross over and walk down **Meadow Close**, where you will find a kissing gate leading to the lake. Turn left to the car park.

PLACES OF INTEREST NEARBY

Irthlingborough Cross
Located on the roundabout junction of Finedon Road, Station Road, and High Street, this preaching cross is thought to date to the 13th century. The 13 feet long shaft is said to have been used as a standard pole for measuring agricultural land.

The National Dragonfly Museum
Housed in an 18th century former mill, the museum is AA-signed from the A605 at Oundle. It is the only dragonfly museum/reserve in Europe, highlighting the plight, beauty, and wonder of dragonflies, of which there are 39 species in Britain. There are exhibitions, videos, and a microscope-TV link. The museum is open on selected weekends in summer. Enquiries: 01832 272427

12 West Haddon and Winwick

Winwick crossroads

The Walk $3\frac{1}{2}$ miles   **Terrain** Undulating farmland and a gated lane
Map OS Landranger 140 Leicester (GR 635715)

How to get there

West Haddon is at the junction of the A428 Northampton–Rugby and the B4036 Daventry–Market Harborough roads. It can be reached from the A14 via Cold Ashby.

Parking At the large car park for patrons of The Pytchley Inn, but no long stays for walking in the evenings, please. There is roadside parking and also by the playing field, which is off the A428, a short distance south-east of the village.

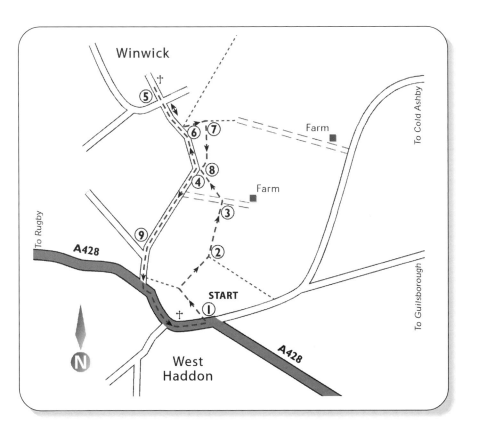

Introduction

Our walk starts off along West Haddon's main street, joining the Jurassic Way to cross undulating farmland and reaching the gated road to Winwick. (In fact you could use the gated road all the way to Winwick and back; it is tarmacked and pleasant, with fine country views and very few vehicles.) Winwick must be on many a list of prettiest places. It is a tiny settlement, consisting of a few cottages, several farms, a 13th century church, and a 16th century manor house. A stream running beside a lane adds to this rural picture. To complete the walk, we do an about-turn and either return directly along the gated road to West Haddon or take a route across short stretches of farmland and a stream before rejoining the gated road.

West Haddon is a thriving village, surrounded by splendid countryside, in the north-west of the county. No less than six roads converge on it now, and in the Middle Ages it was on a drove road, and cattle were rested here on their way south.

Drive and Stroll

Years ago it was more self-sufficient; in the early part of the last century there were several bakehouses. A pony and trap was used for delivery, and one baker offered a roasting service, which I believe was often the case in country villages. The joint with potatoes underneath was taken for the baker to cook and was collected after church. Between the wars this service cost twopence on Sundays and a penny during the week. There was a slaughterhouse, several butchers, a general store, and schools – in fact most facilities – and over the years many alehouses; even today there are three pubs.

These are just a few of the snippets I gleaned from *Milestones and Memories – a stroll through West Haddon*, compiled by the local history group. Other chapters include personal reminiscences which give a good idea of how ordinary people – farmers, tradesmen, and householders – in rural England lived their lives. And with its range of interesting shops available in this new millennium, West Haddon is still a popular place to wander through.

The Pytchley Inn

This impressive-looking building in West Haddon has a rather grand main entrance at the side. The main bar is to the right and here the atmosphere is warm, cosy, and friendly. The Pytchley Inn is well known for its steaks, which include a Pytchley belly buster of 48 oz. Other choices include chicken Tenerife (with garlic butter) and gammon steaks. Snacks and sandwich are available, including freshly filled French bread. Pensioners' meals are served at lunchtime from Monday to Saturday. Telephone: 01788 510426

THE WALK

From the **Pytchely Inn**, turn right along the pavement (West Haddon Post Office and General Stores is almost opposite) and then take the first right into **Crown Lane**. At the far right corner of the cul-de-sac, take the **Jurassic Way and Winwick** footpath. Go through the kissing gate and take the left fork, well-marked underfoot. Walk up to the top of the meadow and follow the footpath round to the right.

At the corner, cross a stile on the left, marked 'Jurassic Way'. Cross farmland now to another stile in the hedgerow. Then the route bears to the left and goes on to the end of a farm track.

Turn left here and bear right along

The Pytchley Inn

a well-defined grassy path to meet up with the gated road.

At the gated road, turn right – at a gate – along the lane towards **Winwick**. Nearing houses on the left, you will see a footpath sign on the right, which is used on the return, but now go ahead along the tarmac lane to the crossroads at Winwick and a white thatched cottage on the right. This is a delightful stretch of walking, with the stream to the left, and it is worth going the short distance to the end of the lane to see the 13th century church.

About turn and backtrack along the lane to the footpath on the left, opposite the houses.

Turn left here. (Alternatively, if you would rather return to West Haddon by the easy walking route, continue along gated road.) Follow the public footpath disc arrow to the right (not the wooden fingerpost). This takes you along the edge of a field bearing left.

Turn right over a footbridge, soon followed by a stile. Cross the next fields, bearing right all the time

Drive and Stroll

along paths, until you cross a stile to join up with the gated road again.

Turn left onto the lane, which is hilly in parts; so don't forget to take a breather from time to time and turn round to admire the views. Carry on past the farmhouse on

the left and turn left into the **Yelverton road**.

At the next junction, turn left into **West End**, making for the village, and at the mini-roundabout, turn left along the A428, back to the Pytchley Inn or your vehicle.

PLACES OF INTEREST NEARBY

Cottesbrooke Hall and Gardens
Situated near Creaton, on A5199, this Queen Anne house has a fine collection of sporting and equestrian pictures, as well as exquisite furniture and porcelain. The gardens were awarded the HHA Christie's Garden of the Year Award 2000. Refreshments are available and there are plants for sale, but dogs are not allowed on the premises. The house and gardens are open on certain days between May and September. Enquiries: 01604 505808; www.cottesbrookehall.co.uk

Coton Manor Gardens, Coton, near Guilsborough
The 10-acre garden was created in the 1920s by the grandparents of the present owner and consists of a series of smaller gardens. Light lunches and homemade teas are available, and there is a specialist nursery. Opening is on certain days between April and October. Enquiries: 01604 740 219; wwwcotonmanor.co.uk

3 Brixworth Country Park and Pitsford Water

A buggy-friendly route

The Walk 3 miles (There are alternative waymarked routes of $^3/_4$ and $^1/_2$ mile - or a $7^1/_2$ mile circuit.)   **Terrain** Mainly surfaced paths with some hilly sections

Maps OS Landranger 141 Kettering and Corby and OS Landranger 152 Bedford and Huntingdon (GR 755695). A leaflet entitled 'Discover Brixworth Country Park' with a detailed map is available from the visitor centre.

How to get there

As you near Brixworth village, follow the brown and white signs from the roundabout on the A508 between the A14 and Northampton. **Parking** At Brixworth Country Park pay-and-display car park. **By bus** A bus service stops at the A508 roundabout $^1/_2$ mile from the visitor centre. (Enquiries: Travelwise, 01604 236464)

Drive and Stroll

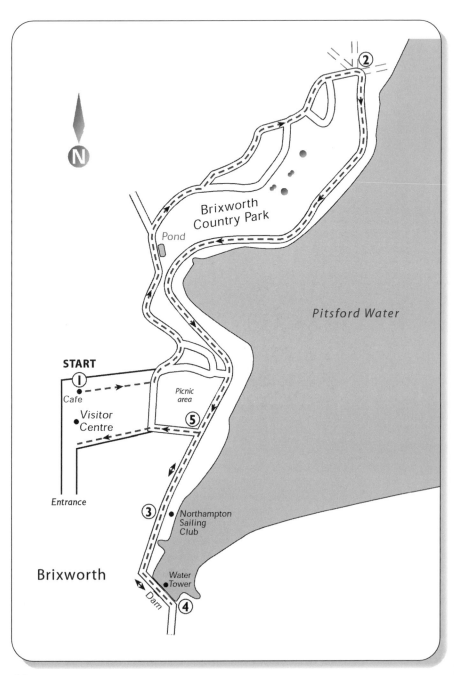

N

Brixworth
Country Park

Pond

Pitsford Water

START
①
Cafe

Visitor
Centre

Picnic
area

⑤

②

Entrance

③ Northampton
Sailing
Club

Brixworth

Water
Tower

Dam

④

Introduction

Starting in Brixworth Country Park by green slopes with wooden sculptures and wide views, our circular route takes us past the sailing club and over the causeway of Pitsford Water. We then retrace our footsteps for a short distance, entering the park again beside the wide grassy picnic area.

Located close to the historic village of Brixworth, the country park is a good place for families, and it can be as lively or as peaceful as you like to make it. You can amble away from the main centre and enjoy the wooden sculptures and seats, the bird hide and pond, or take a picnic and gaze at quite stunning views over Pitsford Water, at the northern end of which is a nature reserve (for admission details, telephone 01604 781350). Alternatively, you may decided to join in one of the events, many of which are suitable for families and people with restricted mobility (for details, telephone 01604 237227). There are hands-on displays at the visitor centre, as well as books and souvenirs. The country park is open every day; the main car park and toilets are open from 9 am to 6 pm from Easter to October and from 9 am to 5 pm from November to Easter. Information: 01604 883920; www.northamptonshire.gov.uk

The Willow Tree Café

The Willow Tree is in Brixworth Country Park and offers light lunches, snacks, ice cream and drinks. There is seating both inside and on a terrace. Telephone: 01604 889343

Or you may like to visit one of the several pubs in Brixworth where refreshments can be had, including the **Coach and Horses** (tel: 01604 880329) and the **George** (tel: 01604 881439). The **White Swan** at Holcot (telephone: 01604 781263) is also close by.

THE WALK

From the Willow Tree Café follow the tarmac path to the left of the car park and past the pond with waterlilies.

(Next, on the left, you could take in a detour around the Sensory Garden, with its interesting sculptures, wind chimes, and a human sun clock [there are instructions!].)

Following the red arrow (**Skylark Trail**) which winds around above Pitsford Water, you'll come to a bird hide up on the left. The next feature on the right is a wooden sculpture, a weather vane, with another pond – and ducks, if you're lucky. Don't turn right past the pond, though, but carry straight on.

Next on the left, look out for a grass maze; all good fun. If you are in need of a rest on this path, along the way there are interesting seats with their backs in the shape

One of the sculptures at Brixworth Country Park

of leaves and hazelnuts. On this gently sloping area there are two footpaths that together on the map look something like a pair of spectacles, the further one being on higher ground. (Although not on our route, it might be fun to wander along these paths, keeping a look out for the interesting wood sculptures, one a pair of binoculars on legs looking out to the water, another depicting points of the compass.)

Finally walk down towards the water and join the main gravel circuit. Watch out for cyclists.

Turn right towards the **Northampton Sailing Club** area. (Ignore the gate

to the right that leads past a pond and back to the visitor centre.) Keep walking forward, past an inlet on the left with gulls and ducks to brighten the way. Then go through a gate and continue along the path behind the sailing boats. Further along, a hedge has been planted on the left, hiding the boats.

At the end of the path turn left, going past the entrance to the sailing club and making for the dam.

From the tarmac road across the dam, look to the left for views across the water to the sailing club and beyond, and at the many waterfowl below. To the right, there is a view of a watercourse and a truly rural scene in undulating countryside.

At the other side of the dam, turn about and retrace your steps, turning right along the path just after the entrance to the sailing club (there's no footpath sign).

Finally, turn left on reaching the path with a signpost pointing back to the visitor centre; that is, unless you feel like continuing on the 7 mile circuit.

The ancient church at Brixworth

PLACES OF INTEREST NEARBY

All Saints' church, Brixworth

Once described as 'perhaps the most imposing architectural memorial of the seventh century surviving north of the Alps' (Sir Alfred Clapham), All Saints' has a long history, with additions and rebuilding taking place over many centuries, and is well worth visiting.

14 Birdwatching at Sywell Country Park

The view from a hide at Sywell

The Walk 3 miles, or a shorter circuit of $2\frac{1}{2}$ miles **Terrain** Easy footpaths and some short slopes
Map OS Landranger 152 Northampton and Milton Keynes (GR 835655) (A leaflet with a map can also be purchased from the visitor centre.)

How to get there

From the A4500 Northampton to Wellingborough road, turn off in the direction of Mears Ashby at the crossroads near Earls Barton and follow the brown and white signs. **Parking** At Sywell Country Park pay-and-display car park. **By bus** A regular bus service stops at Ecton, approximately 1 mile from the park entrance. (Enquiries: Travelwise, 01604 236464)

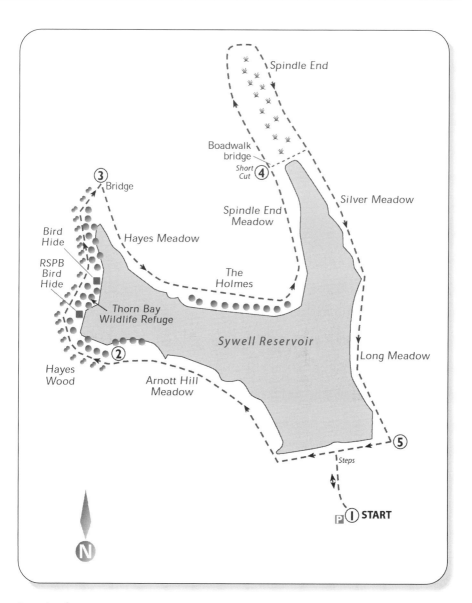

Spindle End

Boadwalk bridge

Short Cut ④

Silver Meadow

③ Bridge

Spindle End Meadow

Bird Hide

Hayes Meadow

RSPB Bird Hide

The Holmes

Thorn Bay Wildlife Refuge

Sywell Reservoir

②

Hayes Wood

Arnott Hill Meadow

Long Meadow

⑤

Steps

P ① START

N

Introduction

This circuit is a mixture of mature woodland, sheep-grazed meadows, and marshland. The reservoir is a refuge for a great variety of birds and waterfowl, and there are two bird hides where they can be observed at close quarters.

Drive and Stroll

In 1983, the county council bought the 68-acre Edwardian reservoir and saved it from becoming a landfill site. The aim was to provide an outdoor amenity for all. Built to supply water to Higham Ferrers and Rushden, the 236 million gallon reservoir and waterworks opened in 1906. Reminders of the reservoir's working past can still be seen: the visitor centre is housed in the original waterworks pumping station and still contains the electric turbine pump. The small arboretum, planted in the 1920s and 30s, was created by the old Water Board. A relatively new addition is Homeopathy Wood.

For me Sywell Country Park is a friendly, relaxing place, which helped me get back on my feet after becoming unfit. At weekends especially, it seemed there was always someone about, usually with a dog, and walkers would pass the time of day or stop for a chat. And if my family came with me, the children could walk along the embankment to feed the ducks (with suitable food) and there's also a children's play area, suitable for children up to 12 years old.

The park is open every day; the car park and toilets are open from 9 am to 5 pm, and the visitor centre from 11 am to 5 pm at the weekend and during school holidays. Details of the special events held there can be obtained from 'People and Places', a free publication available from the visitor centre. Telephone: 01604 810970

Sywell Country Park Visitor Centre

Light refreshments are available here, including hot and cold drinks, ice creams and confectionery. The visitor centre is open from 11 am to 5 pm at weekends and during school holidays.

Alternatively, refreshments can also be found at the **Griffin's Head**, Wilby Road, Mears Ashby (telephone: 01604 812945) and the **World's End**, Ecton (telephone: 01604 414521).

THE WALK

From the car park walk towards the reservoir. Then you have the option of taking the right gravel path to reach the dam or to climb the 67 steps for a little more exercise. Turn left along the embankment, and at the first gate turn right along the hard-surfaced footpath. It may seem obvious, but don't forget to look across the water at the changing views from time to time; this is no plain round pond.

At the entrance to the wildlife refuge, a wooded area, we are reminded to keep dogs on a lead. Carry on ahead along the gravel path and through the woodland. Then, just off the path on the right, is a bird hide overlooking **Thorn Bay**. Returning to the track again, go through **Hayes Wood**. On the right again, is the second hide, which is accessible to wheelchairs and a little more comfortable; there are some useful bird identification charts. Back on track, go through more woodland and continue along the circular path. To the left, open country and cornfields can be seen through gaps in the hedge.

The gravel path stops at the end of the refuge and goes over a small bridge. Turn right onto a grass pathway through **Hayes Meadow**. Keep going ahead and then round a bend into **Spindle End Meadow**.

When you come to the boardwalk bridge over to the right, you can choose either to follow the shorter ($2\frac{1}{2}$ mile) route by crossing the bridge and then turning right, or to continue straight ahead and then round the marshy area named **Spindle End**. The route continues straight ahead, taking you through newly planted **Homeopathy Wood**.

The last stretch is through **Silver Meadow** and then **Long Meadow**. After a dry summer the water level

A quiet moment at Sywell Country Park

gets quite low, and a notice warns of 'very soft mud' and to keep away from the water's edge.

Turn right at the disabled people's car park, towards the valve tower, and then turn left, back to the picnic tables, butterfly garden, play area, toilets, car park, and visitor centre.

PLACES OF INTEREST NEARBY

Sywell Country Park is open all day every day, with the car park and toilets open from 9 am to 5 pm. The visitor centre opens at weekends and school holidays from 11 am to 5 pm. Boules can be hired from the visitor centre (telephone: 01604 810970). Special events are held regularly and details are published in the free guide 'People and Places'.

15 Summer Leys Nature Reserve and Great Doddington

The bridge over the River Nene

The Walk $3\frac{1}{2}$ miles (or 2 miles around the nature reserve)   **Terrain** Easy well-defined paths in reserve; gently undulating across farmland
Map OS Landranger 152 Northampton and Milton Keynes (GR 885635)

How to get there

From A45 near Wellingborough, take the minor road towards Wollaston. **Parking** The free car park at Summer Leys Nature Reserve. **By bus** There is no direct service, but buses run to Great Doddington and Wollaston (01604 236712 (24 hrs) for timetables).

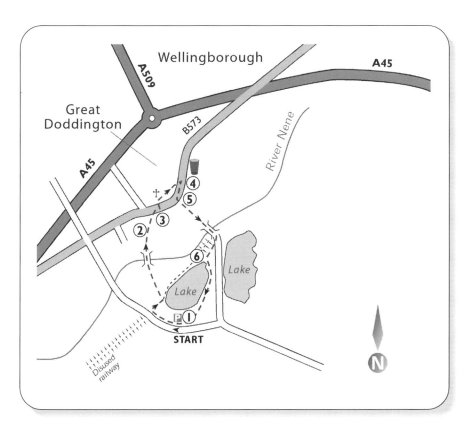

Introduction

The walk sets off in the nature reserve, going across a disused railway line and into pastureland. From there the route goes through the village, and then across fields and past the old mill, which is now a private dwelling. The last part of the stroll takes us back into the reserve. The route is a little more challenging than most in this book, but there is nothing too steep, and the views across the Nene Valley more than compensate for any exertion.

Summer Leys is a relatively new nature reserve, officially opened in 1993. It has been carefully managed to provide a variety of habitats suitable for different types of wildlife: deep and shallow water, marsh, hedgerows, grassland, and trees. A pair of binoculars may be useful, and there are hides overlooking the islands and scrapes.

There has been settlement in the area of Great Doddington at least since the Iron Age, as evidenced by the traces of four hut circles, storage pits, and an internal ditch found there. Saxon and Roman pottery has also been discovered. This long narrow village lies on a limestone ridge overlooking the river Nene and on our walk we can enjoy the marvellous views across the wide valley that many local people get from their gardens. Also on this route is St Nicholas' church, which is partly Norman.

The Stag's Head

The Stag's Head in Great Doddington offers a full à la carte menu in the restaurant, which also serves Sunday lunches. Snacks such as baked potatoes and ploughman's lunches are available. In addition, there is also a children's menu. Food is served every day from 12 noon to 2 pm and from 7 pm to 9.30 pm, or 6.30 pm to 9 pm on Sundays. Dogs are allowed in the small garden but not inside the pub. Telephone: 01933 222316

THE WALK

Looking out to the lakes, take the footpath to the left signed 'Circular Walk 2 miles', which is the shorter route. Our walk follows these discs at the beginning and end. Where the tarmac path turns off right, we take the grassy path parallel with the road bearing left over a wooden bridge. Follow the waymarked route, going even closer to the road and across a bridge. Bear right, still following the circular walk. (Don't be tempted to leave at the corner where new trees are growing, as some people obviously have.) Turn left a little further along, crossing the disused railway line. In front, you will see a wooden bridge, which you cross, and then go over a stile. (Great Doddington can be seen across acres of pastureland to the right.) Walk onwards, making for a single oak tree. Cross the small bridge on the right and go over another stile.

Then follow the public footpath arrow which points along the left of the next field to another stile, that is easily seen. Onwards again and cross a humpback bridge over the river Nene. Go ahead over a stile and keep to the right of this field, with trees and a hedgerow followed by a fence.

On meeting the **Nene Way** sign, turn right over the stile. Walk across the centre of the next field. (You will notice a green shed over to the left, which is not on our route.) Keep walking gradually uphill, keeping to the centre of the field, and then bear left over a stile just before a large green barn. Follow the Nene Way sign through a gate to its right. Go through another iron gate to a smaller white gate in the far right-hand corner, which takes you into **Great Doddington**.

Turn directly right into **Lower Street**.

Turn left into **Chapel Lane** at the the **United Reformed church** and keep onward to the village stores on the right and post office on the left. Cross over the main street; turn right, going past the vicarage, and then left into **Church Lane**. The church of St Nicholas is at the end.

Turn right at a footpath pointer just before the entrance gate. This takes you along behind houses and past the **War Memorial Hall**, a recreation ground, and a livery stable to come out opposite the **Stag's Head** public house.

On the way to Great Doddington

 ④

Turn right, going back along the main street and taking care on the nasty bend. Ignoring the Nene Way paths on the left after the Stag's Head, carry on along the pavement into **High Street**, with a thatched house to the right. At the **Great Doddington village sign**, turn left down **Lower Street**.

 ⑤

Then look out for the **green footpath sign** on the left. Go over the stile – you may be interested in this different type of stile: just a stone slab in the wall to step over – and onto a narrow path between gardens. The footpath soon goes through a kissing gate, from where views across fields, lakes, and river open out. The path and next gate come into view going across a field. At that kissing gate, turn left and go through another kissing gate on a slope. Then walk diagonally to a white farm gate and stile. Rejoin the **Nene Way**, moving onward and down towards the river and a lock. Bear left at the next kissing gate, following the Nene Way arrow, and then walk through another kissing gate; here the route takes us across the front of a former mill and over the lock bridge.

Next, go down the gravel drive and over a bridge, turning right onto the wide, disused railway track.

 ⑥

At the **Summer Leys Nature Reserve** sign, turn left, following the yellow circular discs back to the car park.

16 Harpole Village

The Bull at Harpole

The Walk 4 miles **Terrain** Undulating farmland, with some slight inclines
Map OS Landranger 152 Northampton and Milton Keynes (GR 695605)

How to get there

Harpole is north of the A45 between Daventry and Northampton, just west of Northampton. **Parking** Roadside in the village. The start is in School Lane, near the Old Rectory.

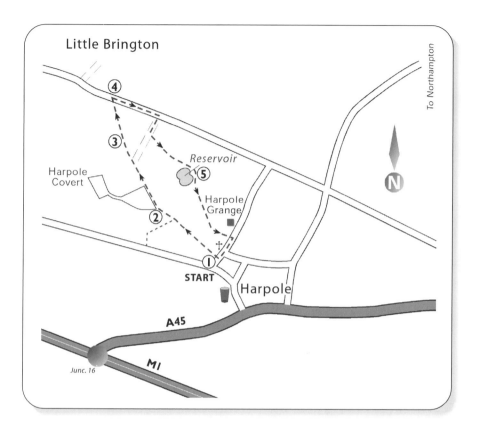

Introduction

For much of the way, the walk is on well-signed tracks through lovely undulating landscape. This is sheep country and dogs should be kept on a lead, especially at lambing time. There are some minor climbs but the variation in altitude is well worth any effort. From Harpole, the circular route sets off into farmland, passing Harpole Covert. A short stretch along the Little Brington–Northampton road marks the start of the return leg, which passes a small reservoir and returns to the village on bridleways and grassy tracks through meadowland.

Harpole – population 1,300 – has become well known for its annual Scarecrow Festival, which takes place over two days, usually early in September; in the order of 10,000 people arrive to watch the celebrations. Most of the inhabitants take part, and hundreds of scarecrows are displayed throughout the village; even the local antiques and clock dealer likes to dress up and frighten his customers.

Drive and Stroll

For people like me, Harpole has also another attraction: Magnus shoe shop, near the church in High Street, specializes in ladies' shoes sizes 9 to 12 and men's size 12 to 16. (Telephone: 01604 831271)

The Bull

The Bull is in High Street, Harpole and is open during usual pub hours. It offers a varied menu, including specials and a children's menu. Telephone: 01604 830666.

THE WALK

From the Old Rectory gate in **School Lane**, turn right, walk to the end of the wall, and turn right at the footpath sign opposite the Methodist chapel. Go through a kissing gate and then, from a farm gate, follow the public footpath sign across a field to another kissing gate, in the far left corner. Bear left slightly and cross another field, going uphill to a kissing gate and not forgetting to take a look at the beautiful surrounding countryside. At the next kissing gate, the public footpath veers to the right of a cluster of trees on the hill. From the top you will see another gate in front (just past a feed trough on my visits). Follow the disc arrow, bearing left uphill to another kissing gate in the corner, and then going down several steps to a farm track.

At the track with a marker post, cut off a corner of the farm track by crossing the field in front of you to 19 steps and a stile. Rejoin the track, turning left and walking beside **Harpole Covert**. Continue straight on to a T-junction. Go straight on here, following the footpath arrows. At the end of the wood, continue ahead, with a hedge on the left and open country to the right. At a solitary oak tree, the route is signed onward and then straight across a junction; the spire of **Little Brington church** should be visible from here. At the end, where the track goes right, we cross a stile with an arrow; then it is just a short way across the corner of the field to reach and go through a wooden gate.

The footpath goes onwards again, with several trees and a hedge on the right. As you near the top of this steepish slope, look out for a stile in the hedge to the right. A sign points left along the edge of this next field, and houses come into view. Go down a dip, over a stile, and through a battered wooden gate. At **Keeper's Cottage**, turn right on the track to arrive at the **Little Brington–Northampton road**.

Someone's watching at Harpole

Turn right along the road for a short distance, taking care. Turn right before the 'national speed limits apply' sign and go through a farm gate, following a bridleway arrow. At the next sign, turn left through a wooden gate and go onto a wide grass bridleway to the left of a field under cultivation; this is a straight, undulating stretch beside fields, which on reaching the tarmac drive continues forward to the locked gates of a small reservoir.

Walk on to the gates. The path goes to the left, following the fence, and at the end bears right towards some trees. In the corner, follow the bridleway sign going between the fence and a hedge. Another bridleway sign then points straight across the next crop field to a wooden gate with no sign; from the gate, the path, which can just be seen in the grass, goes downhill and across another field to a gap in the hedge, where an arrow points ahead across yet another meadow. At the far side, go through a metal gate, on the other side of which is a public bridleway sign that reassures us we are on the right track. Go across another grassy area, through a gate, and finally out to the road.

Turn right along the pavement to the church. For the **Live and Let Live pub**, turn left along **Larkhall Lane**; for the Bull, go past the church and you will find it on the right-hand side round the corner.

17 | Fawsley and Badby

The Windmill at Badby

The Walk 3 to 4 miles **Terrain** Grassland and hard surfaces, with some short steep stretches
Map OS Landranger 152 Northampton and Milton Keynes (GR 565565)

How to get there

Fawsley is approximatley 3 miles south of Daventry. From the A361, turn left (tight) onto a minor road signed to Fawsley. The Knightley Way is signed on the left at the sharp bend after Fawsley Hall. **Parking** At the horse pond near Fawsley Hall and further along, off the sharp bend at the start of the Knightley Way. Parking is limited, especially at weekends and during the bluebell season. **By bus** The service from Daventry and Brackley serves Badby. Saunterbus runs at weekends in summer. (Enquiries: Traveline, 0870 608 2608)

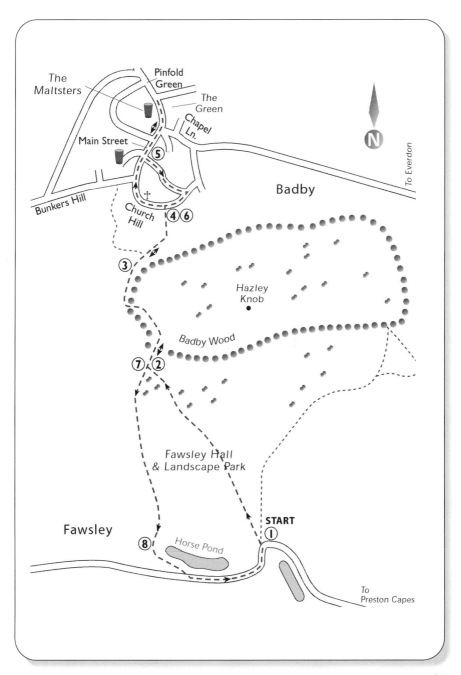

Drive and Stroll

Introduction

This stroll can be taken in either direction: from the little parking area by the horse pond, following the footpath discs, or from the Knightley Way sign. Our route uses the latter. Both incorporate a stretch of road near Fawsley Hall and give an opportunity to take a closer look at St Mary's church. There is some hill walking, which is quite steep for short distances, but the slopes across Fawsley Park can be taken gently.

Fawsley Hall and park was created by the Knightley family, who bought the manor of Fawsley in 1416 and lived there for something like 500 years. After the dissolution of the monasteries in 1539, they also acquired Badby. The site of Fawsley village, which once had a population of around 300 people, lies under the double lakes created by Capability Brown; 12-mile Knightley Way goes between these lakes and on to Greens Norton. Fawsley Hall is now a hotel but the public is allowed to stroll across the landscaped parkland overlooking some of Northamptonshire's prettiest heights. The church of St Mary, just past the hall, contains the Knightley family tombs, including effigies from the 16th century of Sir Richard Knightley and his wife, Jane.

The stone village of Badby has an equally long history, the first known reference dating to 944. It is worth visiting just for a pleasant stroll and perhaps some refreshment. Although the village is probably best known for its walks up to the bluebell wood (or earlier in the year, wood anemones), it was the 'wall to wall' carpet of autumn leaves that left me gasping – or was that the rolling hills of Fawsley? Badby Youth Hostel, the only youth hostel in the county and the only thatched one in England, was once three 17th century cottages which were occupied by Fawsley estate workers.

The Windmill

This is a traditional English pub, situated in the picturesque village of Badby and has been offering hospitality since the 17th century. Amongst its attractions are the first class food in the restaurant, including vegetarian options, and the bar snacks and real ales in the bar. Children and pets are welcome.

THE WALK

Go through the kissing gate signed **'Knightley Way'** and bear slightly left. The paths across this part of the **Fawsley** parkland are signed with large white Knightley Way discs. The grassland gradually slopes upwards and views over this landscaped park and far beyond are well worth any effort.

Go through a kissing gate to the

Fawsley

right leading into **Badby Wood**, where the undulating path goes round the edge for a time.

Keep following the **Knightley Way** signs and at the end of the wood go through a kissing gate into a field. Cross diagonally to another kissing gate. Keep to the left of this field, a perfect and peaceful spot with a glimpse of Badby church to the left and woodland to the right. The path goes through another kissing gate and finally comes out opposite the **church of St Mary the Virgin** in Badby.

At the T-junction, the thatched

YHA building is to the right, but turn left down **Church Hill** towards the **Windmill** public house, followed by the post office, and, further along past the green, the **Maltsters' Arms**.

After exploring the village and admiring the pretty cottages, some with very low doorways, turn about for a short distance and then left into **Vicarage Hill**. Go up to **Church Green** and then turn right, back into **Church Hill**.

Up on a bank to the left, opposite the church, is the wooden fingerpost pointing the way to

Drive and Stroll

Fawsley, which passes between the two houses where we entered the village. Retrace your footsteps along the same footpath to and through **Badby Woods**, taking the right fork leading out of the woods.

At the two kissing gates, leave the **Knightley Way** and bear right. Now a real picture postcard area of the park is crossed. Several paths point downhill to the road and **Fawsley Hall** (which can't be seen from this part of the park). Our route follows the fence on the right, and at another fence, which goes across the meadow, we walk slightly uphill to the left and through a kissing gate with a public footpath sign. Go through the next kissing gate, which is visible from the last. Bear left, following the disc sign across grassland to another kissing gate and a footbridge.

Turn left along the edge of the ploughed field. Don't be tempted to struggle through vegetation to the left, but walk a little further up the slope, and on the left by a horse chestnut tree there is a squeeze stile and disc arrow. From here cross over two more stiles leading back to the road near Fawsley Hall. Turn left if your vehicle is near the bend, and right at the next footpath sign for **St Mary's church**.

PLACES OF INTEREST NEARBY

St Mary's church, Fawsley
Dating to the early 13th century, St Mary's has many fine features, such as carved poppy heads and stained glass thought to be from Sulgrave Manor.

Church of St Mary the Virgin, Badby
Dating mainly from the 14th century, the church was heavily restored in the 1880s. Look out for the cloister windows, Victorian stained glass, and 18th century altar rails.

Badby Wood
Designated a Site of Special Scientific Interest in 1985, this ancient woodland is over 700 years old. It consists predominantly of hazel and oak trees, with ash in wetter areas, as well as a mixture of birch, elder, honeysuckle, holly, and rowan.

18 Stoke Bruerne Wharf and Blisworth Tunnel

On the route from Stoke Bruerne

The Walk $3\frac{1}{2}$ miles **Terrain** Level walking along towpath and across farmland
Map OS Landranger 152 Northampton and Milton Keynes (GR 745505)

How to get there

Stoke Bruerne is south of Northampton, just off the A508. **Parking** At the Canal Museum pay-and-display car park (discount on museum ticket), or by the church (small fee); there is no parking in the village.

Drive and Stroll

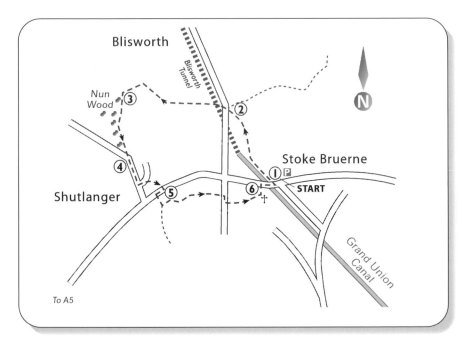

Introduction

This circular route begins with a short stroll along a towpath, passing moored narrowboats with their brightly coloured jugs and flower containers, followed by a stretch across farmland before entering the village of Shutlanger. Passing the church and crossing a humpback bridge, we return by road to Stoke Bruerne lock and the starting point of the walk.

Stoke Bruerne wharf is a package of delights: colourful and bustling on a hot summer's day; quiet and atmospheric out of season. It doesn't seem to matter how many times we watch the activity at this lock and see the narrowboats puttering their way along the canal and into Blisworth Tunnel ($1^3/_4$ miles long), the interest and the tingle along the spine remains the same.

Not that the canal could have been all pleasure for people working the narrowboats in the 1800s; during the winter months, especially, it must have been very tough. The Grand Junction (now the Grand Union) was a trunk route joining the Oxford Canal at Braunston to the Thames at Brentford. There was no Blisworth Tunnel in the early days, and even after it was built there was no towpath for the horses, which had to go over the top. Leggers took the boats through the tunnel by lying on their back and 'walking' sideways along the wall.

Entering the Blisworth Tunnel

The Boat Inn

This inn is situated on the wharf at Stoke Bruerne. It is a popular and interesting inn that has several bars and a restaurant offering a varied menu. Booking is advised at busy times. Telephone: 01604 862428

Or you might like to try **the Old Chapel**, Stoke Bruerne, where morning coffee, lunch, afternoon tea, and dinner are all available. It is a licensed restaurant, and is situated next to the museum car park. There is also **the Plough** at Shutlanger, which is a country pub specializing in seafood. Telephone: 01604 862327

THE WALK

From the car park at the museum, turn right along the towpath towards **Blisworth Tunnel** and away from the lock. Just before the tunnel entrance, take a path to the right going up a slope and continue along the wide pleasant track to arrive at a road.

Turn right towards **Blisworth village**, and shortly turn left onto a bridleway. Go straight on, heading for several trees and a hedge on the right; the path is well worn. Where two hedges meet in a corner – there is a bridleway sign tucked away on your left – turn right along the edge of a field, with the hedge to your right. Follow the

Drive and Stroll

path round the curve and along the next edge of the field in the direction of a wooded area.

 ③

At **Nun Wood** turn left along the signed bridleway beside the trees. At the next arrow sign, turn left; then, almost immediately, turn right towards a barn and the lane.

 ④

At the lane turn left and go into **Shutlanger**. At a large fir tree, turn left into **High Street** and after a dozen or so houses go right into **Baker's Lane**. Carry on, going down a dip with a stream at the bottom and round to the right until you come to the main road, opposite **Water Lane**. (Just along to the right is the **Plough Inn**.)

 ⑤

Carry on into **Water Lane** and turn left through a kissing gate onto a footpath, ignoring the bridleway ahead. Walk across a field to a hedgerow where there is a disc arrow on a telegraph pole. Continue ahead; the route is now well signed over grazing land, through kissing gates, across a footbridge over a stream, and through another gate to a lane. Cross the road and take the footpath along to the right, turning left. The **church of St Mary the Virgin** can be seen at this point. Go ahead but don't go through the churchyard; the footpath bears left, crossing a grassy stretch (the car park) to the road.

 ⑥

Turn right along the pavement into **Stoke Bruerne**, passing the green and some attractive thatched cottages, followed by the **Boat Inn car park**. Go over the humpback bridge to return to the lock and wharf.

PLACES OF INTEREST NEARBY

The Canal Museum, housed in a restored cornmill on the wharf at Stoke Bruerne, tells the story of the inland waterways – these amazing feats of engineering – and the people who worked on them. The museum is open daily in summer, including bank holidays, and in winter, except on Mondays, Christmas Day, and Boxing Day. Telephone: 01604 862229; website: www.thewaterwaystrust.co.uk. Boat trips can be arranged through Stoke Bruerne Boat Co., telephone: 01604 862107.

19 Sulgrave and the American connection

The open countryside near Sulgrave

The Walk 3 miles (with optional extensions to visit the church and old mill) **Terrain** Undulating farmland and quiet lanes
Map OS Landranger 152 Northampton and Milton Keynes (GR 565455)

How to get there

Sulgrave is off the B4525 approximately 7 miles to the north of Brackley. **Parking** Visitors car parks at Sulgrave Manor and the Star Inn; or roadside, possibly in Magpie Road, but please consider residents. **By bus** There is a service on Thursdays from Brackley and Banbury, and Saunterbus and Jason bus services on Sunday during the summer. (Enquiries: Traveline, 0870 608 2608; Jason, 01327 358659)

Drive and Stroll

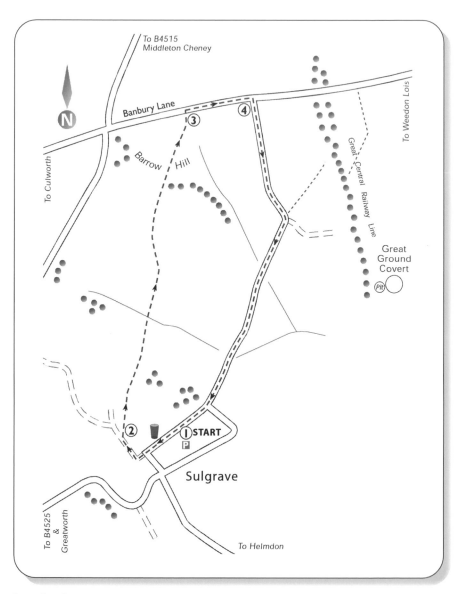

Introduction

Our stroll is a pleasant, well-signed route, passing through meadowland and hayfields before climbing Barrow Hill, the remains of a Bronze Age bowl barrow, built as a funerary monument some 3,000 to 4,000 years ago, with excellent views along the way. After a short stretch along Banbury Lane, we walk down a quiet tarmac lane that was once gated and back to Sulgrave Manor and the village.

Set in open countryside of undulating farmland with ancient hedgerows, this attractive limestone village is probably most famous for its American connections. It is the site of Sulgrave Manor, the Tudor mansion of Lawrence Washington, a 16th century ancestor of George Washington, the first president of the United States; so don't be surprised at hearing an American accent in this tucked away village. The manor is now the headquarters of The Herb Society, which is establishing a large herb garden with many plants that would have been used in the Tudor period. Events such as May Day customs are held there throughout the summer. Except on these special event days, access to the manor is by guided tour only. Memorials to Lawrence Washington, his wife, and son are to be found in the church of St James the Lesser, which dates to the 14th century, although the west tower appears to be earlier: c. 1200.

On the village green are stocks and a whipping post, a 1933 reconstruction using some of the original timber and ironwork. I arrived on Apple Day, an annual celebration of the apple. It was mid-October and the whole village was alive with visitors, which made for a warm, friendly atmosphere, without spoiling the ambience.

The Star Inn

This attractive, ivy-clad 300 hundred year old pub in Manor Road, Sulgrave, offers a warm welcome; the bar is cosy and the seats outside in the sun just made my day. The lunch menu includes grilled sirloin steak with herb butter, roast tomatoes, peas à la française, and chips; ham, egg, and chips; or savoury mince with rice and peas. Telephone: 01295 760389

Alternatively, **at Sulgrave Manor, the buttery** serves light refreshments, tea, coffee, and soft drinks; cakes and biscuits, and picnic tables are available. Telephone: 01295 760205; website: www.sulgravemanor.org.uk

THE WALK

①

If parked at Sulgrave Manor, turn left through the village and go past the **Star Inn** and the apple tree on a tiny green at a road junction. Almost immediately turn right into **Stockwell Lane**.

From the tarmac lane, go through a kissing gate on the right, following a footpath signed '**Northampton circular route**'.

(The lane continues as a bridleway, and, if you fancy the extra walk, turn left for the old mill up on the

Sulgrave stocks

hill. I couldn't resist, but it is a private residence now and there is no public access.)

Cross the short stretch of rough grassland on the diagonal path and then turn left at the gate, following the disc arrow. Still following the signs, go through a farm gate. Bear right across the field – there is a disc on a telegraph pole to follow – turn right over a stile, and then keep to the left of the field, with the hedge on the left. The wide footpath goes down a dip, over a brook, and then onto a grass track beside a meadow. (All I could hear at this point was the rustle of the trees and long grass.)

Go through the next farm gate, and continue onward, past wooded areas on the right and over two plank stiles, the second by a pond. At the grass crossroads, continue

forward; the path then makes for another telegraph pole, with an arrow disc pointing right.

 ③

Shortly, on the left, there is a stile leading to the road, **Banbury Lane**, where we turn right. (There is a grass verge you can step onto if necessary, although on my walk along this lane and the former gated lane I saw only one car and one horse.)

 ④

Disregarding a public footpath sign on the left, turn right down the narrowish, undulating tarmac lane. (There is a seat along the way dedicated to a man on his 80th birthday, which gives a clue to the views along this lane.)

Carry on to **Sulgrave Manor** or the **Star Inn**, perhaps.

20 Cosgrove and the River Great Ouse

A sculpture at Cosgrove

The Walk 3 miles   **Terrain** Mostly level walking
Map OS Landranger 152 Northampton and Milton Keynes (GR 795425)

How to get there

Cosgrove lies on the northwestern outskirts of Milton Keynes, just off the A508. **Parking** Patrons can park at the Barley Mow (if there for any length of time, please park at the end); otherwise on quiet roadsides. **By bus** There are services from Northampton and Milton Keynes. Saunterbus and Jason bus run a Sunday service during the main season. (Enquiries: Traveline, 0870 6082608)

Drive and Stroll

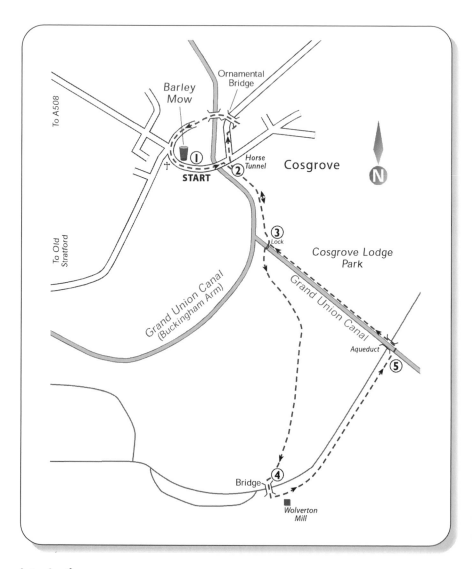

Introduction

Never far away from a watercourse, natural or man-made, this stroll leaves the village of Cosgrove via a horse tunnel to join a canal towpath before branching out across farmland. A restored watermill marks the beginning of the return journey, which follows the river Great Ouse and takes in an aqueduct before rejoining the canal. We retrace our steps through the horse tunnel, with the option of returning directly to the starting point or extending the walk briefly through the village.

When you stroll by the short stretch of the Great Ouse, with herons, reeds, willows, and all the other plants and animals you would expect to see by a mature river, it is difficult to believe that Milton Keynes is just a short distance away. The highlight of the walk for me, the great iron trunk aqueduct, built in 1811 to carry canal traffic over the river Great Ouse, replaced an earlier stone aqueduct which was built in 1805 but collapsed soon after.

The area of Cosgrove with the rivers Great Ouse and Tove attracted settlers in Roman times and beyond. In spite of significant changes with the building of the canal, roads, and motorways, the area has managed to hold on to its rural appeal.

Cosgrove itself is full of historical interest. St Vincent's well behind the old national school in High Street was a holy well, safeguarded by an Act of Parliament. The water is said to have a high iron content, which some believe gives it remedial properties. The Gothic-style stone bridge over the Grand Union Canal was built in the 1790s at the insistence of a local landowner, the huge embankment built to take the canal having cut the village in two.

The Barley Mow

The varied menu at this pleasant, friendly pub in Cosgrove includes ploughman's and sandwiches, as well as steaks, gammon, and other full meals. There is a garden with a large play area and views of the canal. Telephone: 01908 562957

THE WALK

From the Barley Mow, turn left and go through the horse tunnel, which you will see in front of you; it is short and fairly low. Turn right and walk up steps to the **Grand Union Canal**.

Turn left along the towpath, going past Lakeside Store and a caravan park on the left. (Non-residents are not allowed onto the site, but can use the store, which is open in

season.) **Cosgrove lock** soon comes into view at its junction with the Buckingham arm, now disused.

At the lock turn right across the walkway on the lock gate, and directly turn left, following the public footpath; nearby is a wooded area with an intriguing sculpture. The path now goes along the side of a field, moving away from the canal. By an orchard it turns right and then left, over a stile. Now cross the field diagonally – a path can usually be seen – making for a solitary willow tree. Cross the next (large) field, again diagonally, following the disc arrow and making for **Wolverton Mill**, which has been restored and turned into apartments, and the river **Great Ouse**.

Go over the footbridge at **Wolverton Mill** and walk through the grounds. Turn left through a gate into **Ouse Valley Park** and stroll along the side of the river, making for the aqueduct. (The tarmac path goes between the cropped grassy bank of the river and pleasant parkland. Seats at intervals and newly planted trees remind us that this is a park, but a wide area away from the river tells us that we are still in glorious countryside – now just in Buckinghamshire – walking along the bank of a mature river.) Go ahead through a gate; soon the aqueduct comes into sight.

Take the path up to and through a tunnel, turning directly right up the steps. Stroll across the aqueduct and along the towpath, finally going back through the horse tunnel opposite the restored wharf

The iron aqueduct at Cosgrove

buildings. Return to the **Barley Mow**. Alternatively, extend the walk to take in the ornamental bridge by continuing along the towpath as far as the bridge. Cross it and turn left. Go past some houses and turn left again into the Barley Mow.

PLACES OF INTEREST NEARBY

The nearby town of **Stony Stratford** has an ancient history and is well worth exploring. It is here that you will find the Cock and Bull inn, where you can learn the history behind the well-known saying.